T H E   B O O K   O F

Vietnamese
Cooking

THE BOOK OF

Vietnamese
Cooking

DEH-TA HSIUNG

Photographed by
SIMON BUTCHER

HPBooks

ANOTHER BEST SELLING VOLUME FROM HP BOOKS

HPBooks
Published by The Berkley Publishing Group
200 Madison Avenue
New York, NY 10016

9 8 7 6 5 4 3 2 1

ISBN 1-55788-274-6

By arrangement with Salamander Books Ltd.

Home Economist: Lucy Miller
Printed and bound in Spain by Bookprint, S.L.

CONTENTS

INTRODUCTION

Despite centuries of Chinese dominance, Vietnamese culture has maintained its own distinct and highly complex identity, and this is also reflected in its food culture.

It is true that Vietnamese cooking is strongly influenced by the Chinese – from the wok to the chopsticks, and from the quick stir-frying to the wide use of ingredients such as bean sprouts, tofu and noodles – but the similarities are mostly superficial, as the recipes in this book will amply testify.

At first sight, there seems to be very little differences between Vietnamese and Thai cooking, but on closer examination, you will soon discover that partly because of their geographical proximity, the influence of Chinese cuisine is more strongly felt in Vietnam than in Thailand, while the latter seems to have absorbed more influences from the Indian subcontinent.

Obviously there is a certain unity that links the food throughout Southeast Asia: rice is the staple food of this region, and almost every country has extensive coastline with miles of rivers and lakes that yield plentiful supplies of fish and shellfish. Also, large areas of Southeast Asia share a tropical monsoon climate, which makes the lands extremely fertile, providing an abundance of fresh vegetables and fruits all year-round.

——VIETNAMESE COOKING——

The main differences that distinguish Vietnamese cooking from Chinese and all others in Southeast Asia lie not so much in the techniques employed, but more in the emphasis on the use of seasonings – subtlety and lightness of touch being the underlying characteristics that set Vietnamese food apart from all others in this region.

People in the West may not realize that there is an amazing variety of regional cuisine in Vietnam within the context of geography and history: apart from the extensive external influence of China, Vietnam has also a long established vegetarian tradition – derived from Mahayana Buddhism, which originated in India and was

Below: Vietnam hosts an amazing variety of cuisines, from the tropical seafood specialities of the south and the sophisticated vegetarian food of the temperate centre to the less spicy and much more Chinese-influenced stir-fried dishes and clay-pot cooking that are typical of the north of the country.

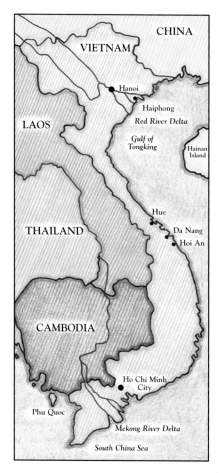

introduced into Indochina by way of China and Thailand. In addition, there is still evidence of the more recent French colonial influence, not to mention the American influence of the 1960s.

Ho Chi Minh City (formerly Saigon) in the south is the most cosmopolitan of all Vietnamese cities and the home of incredible tropical seafood and specialities from the Mekong River delta. With its hot, humid climate and fertile lands, this region also produces a great variety of vegetables, fruits and meats. The French influence is particularly strong here. The small island of Phu Quoc, off the Vietnam/Cambodia border, is reputed to produce the best fish sauce (*nuoc mam*) in Vietnam.

Hue, the former Imperial capital in the centre of the country, has the most sophisticated cuisine and, as the temperate climate is ideal for the cultivation of exotic vegetables, it specializes in vegetarian food.

Hoi An on the central coast was one of the most important ports in Southeast Asia between the 17th and 19th centuries, and Dutch, Portugese, American, Japanese and Chinese merchants all came here.

Hanoi, the capital of Vietnam, is in the north close to the Chinese border. Here the food is less spicy, and the Chinese influence is particularly strong, with stir-fried dishes and clay-pot cooking very much in evidence. The climate is milder here than in the south, and the Red River delta with the Gulf of Tongking produce a wealth of fish and shellfish, as well as vegetables and other foods.

Traditionally, a Vietnamese meal is served with all the dishes, including soup, placed on the table together.

As in China, eating is very much a communal affair. People generally eat in groups, so a number of different dishes can be shared by everyone. An everyday meal consists of 2-3 dishes plus soup and plain rice. Fried rice and noodles do not generally form part of a meal except for a banquet or as a snack. Similarly, no dessert apart from fresh fruit would be eaten after a typical Vietnamese meal. However, almost all the recipes in this book can easily be adapted to be served in Western-style courses.

—EQUIPMENT AND UTENSILS—

Only a very few basic implements are required for Vietnamese cooking and equivalent equipment is very readily available in most Western kitchens: cutting knives and chopping board, pots and pans, spoons and stirrers, sieves and strainers, and so on.

The following list consists of a few essential items:

Pestle and Mortar: Essential item in a Vietnamese kitchen – a blender or food processor can be used instead but will not produce quite the same result.

Knives: A Chinese cleaver is useful though not absolutely essential. A set of sharp kitchen knives of varying sizes is good for Vietnamese cooking.

Wok: A most useful utensil but not absolutely essential – a large frying pan with deepish sides, such as a French sauté pan, is quite adequate.

Steamer: This can be either bamboo or aluminum. If you haven't got a steamer, you can always improvise with a rack or trivet in a wok with a dome-shaped lid.

Saucepans: Several different sizes are a good idea. Pans don't need to be very big, though a large pot for stock making is useful.

Sieves and Strainers: The best type is the bamboo-handled wire "basket" – useful for scooping ingredients such as noodles out of boiling stock or water.

Clay pot: Earthenware pots – hence the name clay pot – are used as casseroles in Vietnamese cooking. The Western versions are usually too large for Vietnamese dishes, so try to get a set of small Oriental clay pots.

Fondue (Hot Pot): Traditionally, a charcoal or spirit-burning Chinese hot pot (also known as a Mongolian fire kettle) is used for table-top cooking. A fondue set is quite adequate.

Chopsticks: The Vietnamese usually use a pair of long bamboo chopsticks for stirring during cooking, rather than a spatula. The standard-size chopsticks that are used for eating are also used in the kitchen for beating, mixing and so on.

—GLOSSARY OF INGREDIENTS—

The following list of ingredients widely used in Vietnamese cooking can be obtained in Oriental grocery stores in the West, and some items are available in supermarkets.

Bamboo Shoots: The young shoots of certain varieties of bamboo, which are pale yellow in color with a crunchy texture. Widely available in cans, some ready sliced. Once opened, rinse in fresh water before use – any unused bamboo shoots can be kept in fresh water in a covered container for up to a week in the refrigerator. **Dried Bamboo Shoots** must be soaked in water for several hours before use.

Banana Leaves: Used for wrapping food to be steamed. Aluminum foil can be used instead, but the food will not have the delicate flavor of the banana leaves.

Basil Leaves: Also known as holy basil, usually sold in bundles, but only the green leaves are used for cooking. They are darker than ordinary sweet basil and spicy with a touch of lemony flavor.

Bean Curd (Tofu): Made of puréed soybeans, this custardlike food is exceptionally high in protein and is virtually cholesterol free. Use the 'firm' rather than the 'soft' type for cooking. **Dried Bean Curd Skins** in sheets or sticks should be soaked in water until soft before use.

Bean Sauce: Made from salted and fermented soya beans, it is available in several types: sweet (see **Hoisin Sauce**), salty and hot, and the colours ranging from red to brown and black. Usually sold in glass jars; once opened, store in the refrigerator.

Bean Sprouts: These are the sprouting shoots of mung beans. Always use fresh sprouts, never canned ones. The sprouts will keep in the refrigerator for 3-4 days. (Not to be confused with bamboo shoots.)

Bean Thread Vermicelli: Also known as **Cellophane** or **Transparent Noodles**, these are fine noodles made from mung beans. Soak in warm water for 10-15 minutes before use.

Black Fungus: Also known as **Tree** or **Wood Ears**, and always sold in dried form. They should be soaked in water for 25-30 minutes, then rinsed in fresh water before use. They have a crunchy texture with a subtle flavor.

Bok Choy: There are 2 basic types widely available in the West – the most common one, with a pale green or yellow color and tightly wrapped elongated head, is known as **Chinese Leaves**. The other variety, known as **Chinese Cabbage,** has a shorter and fatter head with dark green leaves. Both have a white, crunchy stem.

Chiles: Small red 'bird's eye' chiles are less hot than green ones, and they have different flavors too. **Dried Red Chiles** have yet a different flavor. Always wash your hands well after handling fresh chiles and avoid touching the eyes or other sensitive parts of the body.

Chile Sauce: Made from red chiles, vinegar, garlic, salt and sugar, the Vietnamese chile sauce is much more fiery than the standard Chinese chile sauce or the Western hot pepper sauce. So beware!

Chinese (Dried) Mushrooms: Also known as **Black Mushrooms** and **Shiitake Mushrooms** (the Japanese name). They should be soaked in cold water for at least 2 hours or in warm water for 30-45 minutes, then squeezed dry and the hard stalks discarded before use. Fresh mushrooms are no substitute, lacking the intense fragrance and flavor of the dried ones, and the textures are quite different.

Coconut Milk: Not the liquid from the inside of a coconut, but made from dried coconut flesh steeped in boiling water. Used far less often than in Thai cooking. Available in cans and in plastic containers.

Cilantro Leaves: Also known as **Chinese Parsley,** cilantro has a distinctive aroma and is widely used in Vietnamese cooking, as indeed it is throughout Southeast Asia.

Dried Shrimp: Very pungent and quite salty, should be soaked in water before use. See also **Shrimp Paste**.

Fish Sauce: Made from fresh anchovies and salt, an indispensable item for the kitchens throughout Southeast Asia. It is to Vietnamese cooking what soy sauce is to the Chinese. The Vietnamese fish sauce (*nuoc mam*) is not quite the same as Thai fish sauce (*nam pla*) – just as the Japanese soy sauce is different from Chinese soy sauce.

Five-Spice Powder: Another import from China, though not so widely used in Vietnam. It is a mixture of star anise, fennel seeds, cloves, cinnamon bark and Sichuan peppercorns. Some brands have additional spices, such as ginger and coriander seeds, blended with it.

Ginger: Always use fresh ginger root, never the dried powder, which has quite a different flavor. Store in a cool, dark but dry place, not in the refrigerator.

Hoisin Sauce: Also known as Chinese barbecue sauce, it is most versatile – it can be used for dipping and marinating, as well as for cooking. Refrigerate after opening and it will keep for many months.

Lemon Grass: A long, slim bulb with a lemon-citrus flavor – another indispensable item in Vietnamese and Thai cooking. To use, cut off the root tip, peel off the tough outer layers of the stalk, then cut into thin slices before chopping. The stalks will keep for several days in a cool place.

Lily Buds: Also known as **Golden Needles** or **Yellow Flowers** in Chinese, these are the dried buds of the "tiger" lily flower. They should be soaked in warm water for 30 minutes or so, then rinsed in fresh water and the hard tip discarded before use.

Mint: There are many more varieties of mint used in Vietnam than we have in the West, and it is used at almost every meal. For Vietnamese dishes, always use freshly picked leaves, never dried mint.

Noodles: Noodles made from wheat flour known as egg noodles are rarely seen in Vietnam, where only noodles made from rice flour are used. See **Rice Noodles**, below.

Oyster Sauce: Not to be confused with fish sauce – the two are not interchangeable as they are different in flavor and consistency.

Papaya: Use the unripe green papaya for salads or in cooking. When it turns yellow or red, it is eaten as a fruit in Vietnam.

Preserved Vegetable: Also known as **Chinese Preserved Vegetable**, this is pickled mustard greens with roots, and is very salty and hot. It is sold in cans or jars. Once opened, it should be stored under tightly sealed cover in the refrigerator.

Rice: Use the long grain type for everyday meals – the short grain or glutinous rice is only used for special sweet dishes. Thai fragrant rice, also known as jasmine rice, is very popular with Southeast Asian communities in the West. The best way of cooking rice is by microwave or an electric rice cooker. If you do not possess either, then try the following method:

Use 1 cup long grain rice for 4 servings. Wash and rinse in cold water just once, then place the rice in a heavy saucepan with a pinch of salt and 1¼ cups cold water. Cover and bring quickly to a boil. Uncover and stir until almost all the water has evaporated. Reduce the heat to very, very low, cover the saucepan with a tight-fitting lid and cook the rice for 15-20 minutes. Remove from the heat and let stand for 10 minutes or so, then fluff up the rice with a fork or spoon before serving.

Rice Noodles: Also known as **Rice Sticks**, they come in 3 different widths – large, medium and small. There are also very fine strands which are known as **Rice Vermicelli**. They should be soaked in boiling water for 5 minutes or so, then rinsed in cold water to stop them from being overcooked before use.

Rice Paper: Made from rice flour, salt and water, then dried in the sun on bamboo mats. Available as round or large square sheets, they are used for wrapping spring rolls and other foods. The sheets must be dipped in warm water for a few seconds before use.

Rice Vinegar: There are 2 basic types of rice vinegar available: **Red rice vinegar** made from fermented rice is fragrant and mild with a delicate 'sweet' flavor; the distilled **White vinegar** is much stronger with a tangy taste. Cider or sherry vinegar can be substituted.

Sesame Oil: Made from roasted sesame seeds and highly aromatic, it is used for garnishing rather than cooking. The sesame oil made from raw sesame seeds is not suitable for Vietnamese dishes; it needs to be the Oriental variety, which is made with roasted sesame seeds and has a much stronger, nutty flavor.

Shallots: Widely used in Southeast Asia. If unavailable, use the white part of green onions.

Shrimp Paste: Made from fermented dried shrimp with salt, this highly pungent paste is used very sparingly.

Soy Sauce: Used in Vietnam mainly by vegetarians as a substitute for fish sauce. Light soy has more flavor than the dark soy, which has caramel added to give it the rich coloring.

Stocks: In Vietnamese cooking, a simply made chicken stock is used as a base for soups and is added to dishes when a little liquid is required. Use whatever quantity of chicken and/or pork bones (but not beef or lamb) without any skin or too much fat, but a little meat still attached to the bones will improve the flavor. Place the bones in a large pot, cover with cold water and bring to boil, skim off the scum from the surface, then reduce the heat, cover the pot and simmer about 2 hours. Strain and discard bones. Refrigerate when cool, or freeze in small containers if it is not to be used for 4-5 days. A few recipes in this book call for beef stock; to make this, use beef bones, or better still, oxtail, and proceed as above. For vegetarians, use equal amount of dried Chinese mushrooms (with stalks) and fresh bean sprouts, but reduce the cooking time by half. No seasonings are added to the stock as each recipe will have its own. Canned stock or stock cubes are not suitable as they are highly seasoned for Western taste.

Straw Mushrooms: These are grown on beds of rice straw, hence the name. They have a pleasant delicate flavor with an interesting texture. Available in cans.

Tamarind: The pulp and seeds of this acid-flavored fruit are usually sold in sticky brown-black blocks. To make tamarind water, break off a 1-ounce piece, pour over $1\frac{1}{4}$ cups boiling water. Break up the lumps with a spoon, then leave for 30 minutes, stirring occasionally. Strain off the tamarind water, pressing on the pulp; discard the remaining pulp. Also available as a syrup. Lime juice or cider vinegar can be a substitute.

Water Chestnuts: Walnut-sized bulb with brown skin. When peeled, the flesh is white and crisp with a delicate sweet taste. Canned water chestnuts, whole or sliced, are widely available. Once opened, store in fresh water in the refrigerator; they will keep for up to 10-14 days if the water is changed regularly. They are also available fresh from Oriental grocery stores.

SPICY FISH SAUCE

2 cloves garlic
2 small red or green chiles, seeded and chopped
1 tablespoon sugar
2 tablespoons lime juice
2 tablespoons fish sauce

Using a pestle and mortar, pound garlic and chiles until finely ground. If you do not have a pestle and mortar, just finely mince the garlic and chiles.

Place mixture in a bowl and add sugar, lime juice, fish sauce and 2-3 tablespoons water. Blend well. Serve in small dipping saucers.

Makes 4 servings.

Note: This sauce is known as *nuoc cham*. You can make a large quantity of the base for later use by boiling the lime juice, fish sauce and water with sugar in a pan. It will keep for months in a tightly sealed jar or bottle in the refrigerator. Add freshly minced garlic and chiles for serving.

—VEGETARIAN DIPPING SAUCE—

1 tablespoon sugar
2 tablespoons chile sauce
2-3 tablespoons water
1 small red or green chile, seeded and chopped
1 tablespoon roasted peanuts, coarsely chopped

In a small bowl, mix the sugar with the chilesauce and water.

Add chopped chile and transfer the sauce to 4 individual saucers to serve. Sprinkle the chopped peanuts over the top as a garnish.

Makes 4 servings.

Note: This sauce is known as *nuoc leo*. The liquid base can be made in advance; add the freshly chopped chile and the peanuts just before serving.

──── SWEET & SOUR SAUCE ────

2 tablespoons vegetable oil
1 clove garlic, chopped
2 shallots or ½ onion, chopped
1 teaspoon chile sauce
2 tablespoons tomato sauce
2 tablespoons soy sauce
1 tablespoon fish sauce
2 tablespoons sugar
2 tablespoons red rice vinegar
About ½ cup chicken broth
2 tablespoons cornstarch

Heat oil in a medium saucepan and gently
stir-fry the garlic and shallots or onion until
golden but not brown.

Add chile sauce, tomato sauce, soy and fish
sauces, sugar and vinegar. Stir to blend well,
then add the broth and bring to a boil, stirring continuously.

Taste the sauce to check the sweet and sour
balance, and adjust seasoning if necessary.
Mix cornstarch with 2-3 tablespoons water
and add to sauce, stirring until smooth, then
remove from heat and serve.

Makes about 2 cups.

Note: This sauce is traditionally used for
fried or grilled dishes, or it can be used as a
dip at the table.

——VIETNAMESE HOT SAUCE——

1 clove garlic, chopped
2 small red or green chiles, seeded and chopped
1 teaspoon finely chopped ginger root
1 tablespoon chile sauce
2 sticks lemon grass, peeled and chopped
2 tablespoons vegetable oil
2 tablespoons soy sauce
1 tablespoon fish sauce
2 tablespoons sugar
2 tablespoons lime juice with pulp
4-6 tablespoons chicken broth or water
2 tablespoons chopped fresh cilantro leaves
1 tablespoon cornstarch

Using a pestle and mortar, pound the garlic, chiles, ginger, chile sauce and lemon grass to a paste. Heat oil in a medium saucepan and gently stir-fry the paste with soy sauce, fish sauce, sugar, lime juice and broth or water, then bring to a boil.

Blend in chopped cilantro. Mix cornstarch with 2 tablespoons water and stir the paste into the sauce to thicken it. Remove from heat and serve.

Makes about 1½ cups.

Note: This highly spiced sauce goes well with all sorts of meat or fish dishes – it can form the base for curry sauce, or it can be served as a dip.

CARROT FLOWERS

1 long carrot, about inch in diameter

Use a small sharp knife to make a cut towards the pointed end of the carrot, to form a petal-shape about ¼ inch wide. Repeat cuts around the carrot to form a flower with 4 petals.

Angle the knife in such a way that with a slight twist, the flower comes away from the carrot. Repeat this process along the length of the carrot.

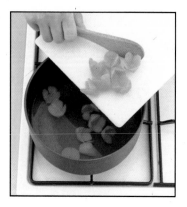

Drop the flowers into a pan of boiling salted water for about 1 minute, to improve the color. Drain and rinse in cold water. Dry well. Use as a garnish, singly or in clusters.

GARNISHES

2 small firm tomatoes
6-8 radishes
4 green onions, white parts only
4 small red or green chiles, seeded

To make tomato roses, use a small sharp knife to peel off the skin, like an apple, in one piece. Curl the skin into a circle, then invert it to form a rose.

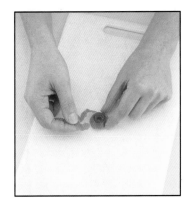

To make radish flowers, cut thin petals all the way round each radish, starting at the root and finishing at the top. Plunge them into iced water and leave for 1 hour or so; the petals will open up to form a flower. Drain and pat dry before use.

To make green onion and chile flowers, make fine cuts about halfway along the length of the vegetables to form fine petals. Place in a bowl of iced water and leave for 5-10 minutes; they will open up to form curly flowers. Dry well before using them as garnishes.

—VIETNAMESE SPRING ROLLS—

FILLING
2 oz. bean thread vermicelli, soaked then cut into
   ½-inch pieces
2 tablespoons black fungus, soaked then coarsely
   chopped
8 oz. ground pork
4 oz. raw peeled shrimp, chopped
1 small onion, finely chopped
2 green onions, finely chopped
1 teaspoon finely chopped garlic
2 tablespoons fish sauce
Salt and freshly ground black pepper
ASSEMBLING AND FRYING
10-12 sheets dried rice paper
1 egg, beaten
Oil for deep-frying

Combine the filling ingredients in a medium
bowl. Set aside. Soften the rice papers, one
at a time. If using square ones, cut each in
half; if using round ones, leave whole. Place
about 2 tablespoons of the filling at one end
of the paper, fold over and tuck in both sides
and roll over. Seal the end with a little
beaten egg and set aside. Repeat to fill all
the rolls.

Heat the oil in a wok or deep-fat fryer to
about 350F (180C) and deep-fry the rolls, in
batches, 5-7 minutes until golden brown.
Remove and drain. (If they are not to be
served at once, they can be kept in a very
low oven up to 3 hours until needed.

SERVING ACCOMPANIMENTS
Iceberg or leaf lettuce
Fresh mint and cilantro leaves
Spicy Fish Sauce, page 14

Separate the lettuce into single leaves and arrange on a serving platter with the mint and cilantro leaves.

Cut the cooked spring rolls in half and arrange on the platter with the lettuce leaves, mint and cilantro leaves. Place a saucer of the Spicy Fish Sauce in the center for dipping. (The dipping sauce can be served in individual saucers, if preferred.)

To serve, place half a spring roll with a mint and cilantro leaf on a lettuce leaf, then wrap it into a neat parcel. Holding it with fingers, dip into the fish sauce before eating.

Makes 4-6 servings.

Variation: To make vegetarian spring rolls, substitute 8 oz. bean sprouts, 1 grated carrot and 1 (8- oz.) cake tofu for the pork and shrimp. Serve with Vegetarian Dipping Sauce, page 15, instead of the fish sauce.

——SHRIMP CRYSTAL ROLLS——

8 oz. cooked peeled shrimp
4 oz. cooked pork, coarsely chopped
4 oz. cooked chicken meat, coarsely chopped
2 tablespoons grated carrot
2 tablespoons chopped water chestnuts
1 tablespoon chopped preserved vegetable
1 teaspoon finely chopped garlic
2 green onions, finely chopped
1 teaspoon sugar
2 tablespoons fish sauce
Salt and freshly ground pepper
10-12 sheets dried rice paper
Flour and water paste
Fresh mint and cilantro leaves
Iceberg or leaf lettuce leaves
Spicy Fish Sauce, page 14

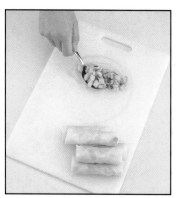

Cut any large shrimp in half. In a bowl, mix shrimp, pork, chicken, grated carrot, water chestnuts, preserved vegetable, garlic, onions, sugar, fish sauce, salt and pepper. Fill a bowl with warm water, then dip the sheets of rice paper in the water one at a time. If using large sheets of rice paper, fold in half then place about 2 tablespoons of the filling onto the long end of the rice paper, fold the sides over to enclose the filling and roll up, then seal the end with a little of the flour paste. The roll will be transparent, hence the name crystal.

To serve, place some mint and cilantro in a piece of lettuce leaf with a crystal roll and wrap into a neat parcel, then dip the roll into the Spicy Fish Sauce before eating.

Makes 4 servings.

—QUAIL WRAPPED IN LETTUCE—

8-10 oz. quail meat, boned and minced
Salt and freshly ground black pepper
½ teaspoon sugar
2 teaspoons fish sauce
3 tablespoons vegetable oil
½ teaspoon minced garlic
½ teaspoon minced ginger root
1 tablespoon chopped green onion
2 tablespoons chopped Chinese mushrooms, soaked
2 tablespoons chopped water chestnuts
1 tablespoon chopped preserved vegetable
2 tablespoons oyster sauce
12 iceberg or leaf lettuce leaves
Fresh mint and cilantro leaves
Spicy Fish Sauce, page 14

In a bowl, mix quail meat with salt, pepper, sugar and fish sauce and marinate 15-20 minutes. Heat the oil in a wok or frying pan and lightly brown the garlic and ginger. Add quail meat and stir-fry for about 1 minute. Add onion, mushrooms, water chestnuts and preserved vegetable and blend well. Stir-fry 2 minutes, then stir in the oyster sauce. Transfer to a serving dish.

To serve, place 2 tablespoons of mixture on a lettuce leaf with some mint and cilantro and roll it up tightly, then dip the roll into the Spicy Fish Sauce before eating.

Makes 4-6 servings.

Variation: Pigeon, duck or other game birds can be cooked and served in the same way.

SHRIMP PASTE ON SUGAR CANE

14 oz. raw peeled shrimp
2 oz. fresh fatty pork, chopped
½ teaspoon chopped garlic
Salt and freshly ground black pepper
1 teaspoon sugar
1 tablespoon cornstarch
1 egg white, beaten
12-inch section of sugar cane
Cilantro leaves, to garnish
Spicy Fish Sauce, page 14

Using a pestle and mortar, pound shrimp, pork and garlic to a smooth paste. Mix with the salt, pepper, sugar, cornstarch and egg white, making sure the paste is well blended.

Preheat broiler. Peel the sugar cane, cut it into 4-inch lengths and split lengthwise into quarters. Mould the shrimp paste onto the sugar cane, leaving about 1-inch of sugar cane at one end uncovered, to use as a handle.

Broil the sticks under the moderately hot broiler 5-6 minutes, turning to ensure even cooking. Garnish with cilantro. To serve, dip each stick in the Spicy Fish Sauce before eating. When the shrimp paste is eaten, the sugar cane can be sucked and chewed.

Makes 4-6 servings.

Variation: Instead of broiling, the sugar cane can be deep-fried in hot oil 4-5 minutes until golden brown.

SESAME SHRIMP TOASTS

8-10 oz. raw peeled shrimp, chopped
½ teaspoon minced garlic
½ teaspoon finely chopped ginger root
2 shallots or 1 small onion, finely chopped
1 egg, beaten
Salt and freshly ground black pepper
1 tablespoon cornstarch
1 French baguette
3-4 tablespoons white sesame seeds
Oil for deep-frying
Chopped fresh cilantro leaves, to garnish

In a bowl, mix the shrimp, garlic, ginger, shallots, egg, salt, pepper and cornstarch and chill in the refrigerator for at least 2 hours.

Cut the bread into ½-inch slices and spread thickly with shrimp mixture on one side, then press that side down onto the sesame seeds so that the entire surface is covered by the seeds, making sure the seeds are firmly pressed into the shrimp mixture.

Heat the oil in a wok or deep-fat fryer to 350F (180C) and deep-fry the toasts, in batches, spread-side down, 2-3 minutes until they start to turn golden brown around the edges. Remove and drain on paper towels. Serve hot, garnished with chopped cilantro leaves.

Makes 6-8 servings.

DEEP-FRIED FISH BALLS

1 lb. firm white fish fillet, skinned
4 oz. potato flour
¼ cup coconut milk or water
Salt and freshly ground black pepper
1 tablespoon chopped cilantro leaves
½ teaspoon minced garlic
1 egg, beaten
Flour for dusting and oil for deep-frying
Lettuce leaves, to garnish
Spicy Fish Sauce, page 14

Remove bones from fish, then cut into small pieces. Using a pestle and mortar, pound to a paste with potato flour and coconut milk, adding the coconut milk a little at a time.

In a medium bowl, mix the fish paste with the salt, pepper, chopped cilantro, garlic and egg. Blend well, then shape the mixture into about 20-24 small balls, dusting with flour.

Heat the oil in a wok, frying pan or deep-fat fryer to 350F (180C) and deep-fry the fish balls, in batches, 3-4 minutes or until golden brown. Remove and drain. Serve on a bed of lettuce leaves with the Spicy Fish Sauce as a dip.

Makes 8-10 servings.

Variation: Other types of seafood such as shrimp, squid and crabmeat can be cooked in the same way.

──SQUID WITH SPICY CHILES──

1 lb. fresh squid, cleaned
½ teaspoon minced garlic
½ teaspoon chopped ginger root
Salt and freshly ground black pepper
1 tablespoon fish sauce
2 tablespoons vegetable oil
2 green onions, finely shredded
3-4 small red chiles, seeded and sliced
Cilantro leaves, to garnish

Pull the head off each squid, discard head and transparent backbone, but reserve the tentacles. Cut open the body and score the inside of the flesh in a criss-cross pattern.

Cut the squid into small pieces about 1 x 1½ inches. Blanch the squid and the tentacles in a saucepan of boiling water 1 minute only – cooking for any longer will toughen the squid. Remove and drain, then dry well. Mix garlic, ginger, salt, pepper and fish sauce in a bowl, add blanched squid and marinate 25-30 minutes.

Meanwhile, heat the oil in a small saucepan until hot but not smoking. Remove the pan from the heat, add green onions and chiles and let stand 15-20 minutes. Arrange the squid with the marinade on a serving plate, pour the oil with the green onions and chiles all over the squid and garnish with cilantro leaves. Serve cold.

Makes 4-6 servings.

SEAFOOD SKEWERS

12 scallops
12 large raw peeled shrimp
8 oz. firm white fish fillet, such as halibut, cod or
    monkfish, cut into 12 cubes
1 medium onion, cut into 12 pieces
1 red or green bell pepper, cut into 12 cubes
½ cu) dry white wine or sherry
1 tablespoon chopped dill
1 tablespoon chopped holy basil leaves
1 tablespoon lime juice or vinegar
Salt and freshly ground pepper
Vegetable oil for brushing
Spicy Fish Sauce, page 14, to serve

In a bowl, mix scallops, shrimp, fish, onion
and bell pepper with the wine, dill, basil,
lime juice or vinegar, salt and pepper.
Marinate in the refrigerator 2-3 hours, the
longer the better. Meanwhile, soak 6 bamboo skewers in hot water 25-30 minutes and
preheat grill or broiler. Thread seafood and
vegetables alternately onto the skewers so
that each skewer has 2 pieces of every
ingredient.

Brush each filled skewer with a little oil and
grill or broil 5-6 minutes, turning frequently.
Serve hot with the fish sauce as a dip.

Makes 6 servings.

——————CHICKEN SATAY——————

1 lb. chicken breast, cut into 1-inch cubes
1 teaspoon minced garlic
2 shallots or 1 small onion, finely chopped
1 tablespoon ground coriander
1 teaspoon sugar
1 tablespoon mild curry powder
2 tablespoons fish sauce
1 tablespoon lime juice or vinegar
Salt and freshly ground black pepper
Vegetable oil for brushing
Chopped onion and cucumber, to garnish
Roasted peanuts, crushed and mixed with
    Vietnamese Hot Sauce, page 17, to serve

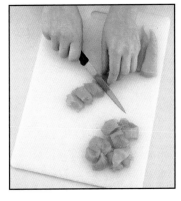

In a bowl, mix chicken with garlic, shallots or onion, coriander, sugar, curry powder, fish sauce, lime juice or vinegar, salt and pepper, then marinate 2-3 hours. Meanwhile, soak 16 bamboo skewers in hot water 25-30 minutes. Preheat grill or broiler.

Thread 4 chicken cubes on to one end of each skewer. Brush each filled skewer with a little oil and grill or broil 5-6 minutes, turning frequently. Garnish with the chopped onion and cucumber, and serve hot with the sauce as a dip.

Makes 8 servings.

Variation: Pork fillet, beef steak or lamb can be prepared and cooked in the same way.

──MONGOLIAN-STYLE LAMB──

2 cloves garlic, chopped
1 tablespoon chopped ginger root
2 shallots or white part of 3 green onions, chopped
1 tablespoon five-spice powder
Salt and freshly ground black pepper
1 teaspoon chile sauce
2 tablespoons fish sauce
1½ lbs. leg of lamb fillet, boneless
12-16 crisp lettuce leaves
Fresh mint and cilantro leaves
Spicy Fish Sauce, page 14

With pestle and mortar, pound garlic, ginger and shallots to a paste. Mix with five-spice powder, salt, pepper, chile and fish sauces.

Cut lamb fillet into 6 long strips. Rub the spice mixture all over the lamb strips and marinate in the refrigerator 3-4 hours. Pack the meat, with the marinade, in a heatproof dish or bowl. Place in a steamer and steam over high heat 2-3 hours.

Preheat grill or broiler. Remove meat strips from steamer and grill or broil them 3-4 minutes, turning frequently so that they are slightly charred but not burned. Pull the meat into small shreds and wrap in the lettuce leaves with some mint and cilantro. Dip the rolls in the Spicy Fish Sauce before eating.

Makes 6-8 servings.

─────SPICY SPARERIBS─────

1 teaspoon minced garlic
2 small red chiles, seeded and finely chopped
1 tablespoon finely chopped lemon grass
2 teaspoons five-spice powder
1 tablespoon sugar or clear honey
Freshly ground black pepper
1 tablespoon fish sauce
3 tablespoons hoisin sauce
12 pork spareribs, trimmed of excess fat
About ¾ cup broth or water
Sweet & Sour Sauce, page 16, and/or Vietnamese
    Hot Sauce, page 17, to serve

Using a pestle and mortar, pound the garlic, chiles and lemon grass to a fine paste.

Mix in the five-spice powder, sugar or honey, pepper, fish and hoisin sauces to make a smooth paste. Coat the spareribs with the mixture and marinate in the refrigerator 3-4 hours, the longer the better.

Preheat oven to 425F (220C). Spread out the ribs in a baking dish. Blend the broth or water with the marinade and pour it over the ribs. Cook in oven 25 minutes, then reduce heat to 350F (180C) and turn the ribs over. Baste with the marinade and cook 25-30 minutes, until tender. Serve hot with the Sweet and Sour Sauce and/or the hot sauce as a dip. Garnish with cilantro, if desired.

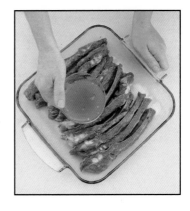

Makes 6-8 servings.

——SPICY CHICKEN SALAD——

8-10 oz. boneless cooked chicken meat, shredded
½ cucumber, thinly shredded
1 carrot and 1 small onion, thinly shredded
Salt and freshly ground black pepper
Few lettuce leaves
2 small red chiles, seeded and shredded
1 tablespoon roasted peanuts, crushed
Cilantro leaves, to garnish
DRESSING
1 clove garlic, chopped
1 teaspoon chopped ginger root
1-2 small red or green chiles, chopped
1 tablespoon sugar
2 tablespoons each fish sauce and lime juice
1 tablespoon sesame oil

In a bowl, mix together chicken, cucumber, carrot and onion and season with salt and pepper. Arrange a bed of lettuce leaves on a serving dish or plate and spoon the chicken mixture on top.

For the dressing, using a pestle and mortar, pound the garlic, ginger, chiles and sugar to a fine paste, then blend the paste with the rest of the dressing ingredients. Pour the dressing all over the salad just before serving, and garnish with the chiles, peanuts and cilantro leaves.

Makes 4-6 servings.

Note: Do not toss and mix the salad with the dressing until ready to serve.

—GREEN PAPAYA SALAD—

1 small unripe green papaya, peeled and thinly
   shredded
1 large or 2 small carrots, peeled and thinly
   shredded
Salt and freshly ground black pepper
Few lettuce leaves
1 tablespoon crushed roasted peanuts, to garnish
DRESSING
1 clove garlic, chopped
1 shallot, chopped
2 small red or green chiles, seeded and chopped
1 tablespoon dried shrimp, soaked and rinsed
2 teaspoons sugar
3 tablespoons lime juice or vinegar
2 tablespoons fish sauce

Mix the shredded papaya and carrot with
salt and pepper. Arrange a bed of lettuce
leaves on a serving dish and pile the papaya
and carrot on top. For the dressing, using a
pestle and mortar, pound the garlic, shallot,
chiles, shrimp and sugar to a fine paste.
Blend with the lime juice or vinegar and the
fish sauce to make the dressing.

Garnish the salad with the crushed peanuts
and pour the dressing all over it. Do not toss
or mix the salad until at the table and ready
to serve.

Makes 4-6 servings.

Note: This salad can be served either as a
starter or as a side dish with main courses.

PICKLED CUCUMBER

1 cucumber, unpeeled, halved lengthwise, then cut
  into thin slices
1 large or 2 small carrots, peeled and thinly sliced
2 shallots or 1 small onion, chopped
4-6 small dried red chiles
2 teaspoon salt
1 tablespoon sugar
2 tablespoons rice vinegar
1 tablespoon fish sauce
GARNISH
1 tablespoon chopped fresh cilantro leaves
1 tablespoon crushed roasted peanuts

Combine cucumber, carrots, shallots or
onion and chiles with salt, sugar, vinegar
and fish sauce in a sealed jar or container.
Mix well and marinate in the refrigerator 4-
6 hours.

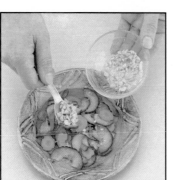

Garnish the pickles with chopped cilantro
and crushed peanuts, and serve either as a
relish or as a side dish with main courses.

Makes 4-6 servings.

Variation: Other vegetables such as celery,
cabbage, green beans, green and red bell
peppers and leeks can be cut into small
pieces and pickled in the same way – allow a
longer pickling time, 4-5 days in the refrigerator.

——HOT & SOUR SHRIMP SOUP——

1 teaspoon chopped ginger root
1 tablespoon chopped lemon grass
2-3 small fresh red chiles, seeded and chopped
3 cups chicken broth
2-3 tablespoons lime juice or vinegar
3 tablespoons fish sauce
1 tablespoon dried shrimp, soaked and rinsed
1 (8-oz.) cake tofu, cut into small cubes
1 oz. bean thread vermicelli, soaked and cut into
    short lengths
2 tablespoons soaked black fungus, coarsely chopped
¼ cucumber, thinly shredded
4-6 oz. cooked peeled shrimp
Salt and freshly ground white pepper
Cilantro leaves, to garnish

Using a pestle and mortar, pound the ginger,
lemon grass and chiles to a fine paste. Bring
the broth to a rolling boil in a pan, add the
lemon grass mixture with the lime juice or
vinegar, fish sauce and dried shrimp. Bring
back to a boil, then add tofu, vermicelli and
black fungus. Simmer mixture about 2
minutes.

Add cucumber and shrimp, bring back to a
boil once more, then season with salt and
plenty of pepper. Serve the soup hot (see
Note), garnished with cilantro leaves.

Makes 4-6 servings.

Note: This soup must be served piping hot –
warm both serving tureen and soup bowls.

SEAFOOD SOUP

1 tablespoon vegetable oil
½ teaspoon minced garlic
2 small fresh red chiles, seeded and chopped
1 tablespoon chopped onion
3 cups chicken broth
8 oz. squid, prepared as for Squid with Chiles,
     page 27
4 oz. fresh scallops, sliced
4 oz. raw peeled shrimp
2-3 tablespoons lime juice or vinegar
1 tablespoon sugar
3 tablespoons fish sauce
8 oz. bean sprouts
¼ cucumber, thinly shredded
Salt and freshly ground black pepper
Cilantro leaves, to garnish

Heat the oil in a wok or pan over high heat and lightly brown garlic, chiles and onion. Add broth and bring to a rolling boil. Stir in the squid, scallops, shrimp, lime juice or vinegar, sugar and fish sauce. Simmer 2 minutes.

Add bean sprouts and shredded cucumber, bring back to a boil and adjust the seasoning. Serve the soup piping hot, garnished with cilantro leaves.

Makes 4-6 servings.

Note: The seafood and vegetables must not be overcooked, or the seafood will be tough and the vegetables lose their crispiness.

──VIETNAMESE FISH SOUP──

1 tablespoon vegetable oil
2 cloves garlic, finely chopped
2 shallots or 1 small onion, chopped
1 tablespoon each chile sauce and tomato paste
2 medium tomatoes, cubed
3 tablespoons fish sauce
2 tablespoons sugar
3 cups chicken broth
2 tablespoons tamarind water or lime juice
8 oz. firm fish fillet, cut into small slices
4 oz. fresh scallops, sliced
4 oz. raw peeled shrimp
12 clams or mussels, scrubbed clean
2-3 tablespoons dry white wine or sherry
Salt and freshly ground black pepper
Cilantro leaves, to garnish

Heat oil in a wok or pan and lightly brown garlic and shallots or onion. Add the chile sauce, tomato paste, cubed tomato, fish sauce and sugar. Blend well, then simmer mixture 2-3 minutes. Add the broth with tamarind water or lime juice and bring to a boil.

When ready to serve, add the seafood and wine or sherry to the broth, bring back to a boil, cover and simmer 3-4 minutes until clam or mussel shells have opened; discard any that remain closed after cooking. Taste soup and adjust the seasoning. Serve hot, garnished with cilantro leaves.

Makes 4-6 servings.

Note: Take care not to overcook seafood. If using already-shelled clams or mussels, reduce the cooking time by half.

CHICKEN SOUP

1 tablespoon vegetable oil
½ teaspoon minced garlic
2 shallots or 1 small onion, thinly sliced
3 cups chicken broth
   8 oz. cooked chicken meat, boned and thinly
   shredded
1 oz. bean thread vermicelli, soaked then cut into
   short lengths
1 tablespoon black fungus, soaked and cut into small
   pieces
12-16 lily buds, soaked and trimmed
2 tablespoons fish sauce
Salt and freshly ground black pepper
2-3 green onions, sliced
Cilantro leaves, to garnish

Heat oil in a wok or pan over medium heat and stir-fry garlic and shallots or onion until aromatic; do not brown them. Add chicken broth and bring to a boil. Add the chicken, vermicelli, fungus, lily buds and fish sauce, bring back to a boil, reduce heat and simmer about 3 minutes.

Taste and adjust the seasoning, then add the green onions. Serve the soup hot, garnished with cilantro leaves.

Makes 4-6 servings.

Variation: If cooked chicken is not available, raw chicken fillet can be used instead, but increase the cooking time by at least 2 minutes, or until chicken is cooked.

——PAPAYA & PORK SOUP——

4½ cups chicken broth or water
4 pork chops, each weighing about 3 oz.
1 small unripe green papaya, peeled and cut into
   small cubes
2 tablespoons fish sauce
Salt and freshly ground black pepper
1 tablespoon chopped green onions
Cilantro leaves, to garnish

Bring broth or water to a boil in a wok or
pan over high heat and add the pork. Bring
back to a boil and skim off the scum. Reduce
heat, cover and simmer 25-30 minutes.

Add the papaya cubes and fish sauce, bring
back to a boil and cook the soup 5 minutes.

To serve, place salt, pepper and the chopped
green onions in a tureen. Pour the boiling
soup with its content over it, garnish with
cilantro leaves and serve at once. The pork
should be so tender that one can easily tear
it apart into small pieces for eating.

Makes 4 servings.

——VIETNAMESE BEEF SOUP——

6-8 oz. beef steak, thinly sliced
¼ teaspoon freshly ground black pepper
½ teaspoon minced garlic
½ teaspoon sugar
2 teaspoons soy sauce
1 tablespoon vegetable oil
1 teaspoon finely chopped lemon grass
2 shallots, thinly sliced
3 cups beef or chicken broth
1 tablespoon fish sauce
Salt to taste
GARNISH
2 green onions, chopped
Chopped cilantro leaves

In a bowl, marinate the beef slices with the pepper, garlic, sugar and soy sauce in the refrigerator at least 2-3 hours. Heat oil in a wok or pan and stir-fry chopped lemon grass and shallots for about 1 minute. Add beef or chicken broth and bring to a boil.

Add the beef and fish sauce and bring back to a boil. Adjust seasoning and serve at once, garnished with chopped green onions and cilantro.

Makes 4 servings.

——MIXED VEGETABLE SOUP——

1 tablespoon vegetable oil
1 teaspoon minced garlic
1 small onion, chopped
1 teaspoon chile sauce
1 tablespoon sugar
3 cups vegetarian broth or water
2 tablespoons soy sauce
3 tablespoons tamarind water or 2 tablespoons lime
   juice
1 (8-oz.) cake tofu, cut into small cubes
8 oz. bok choy (Chinese cabbage) or spinach,
   chopped
6 oz. bean sprouts
3-4 firm tomatoes, cut into thin wedges
Salt and freshly ground black pepper
5-6 fresh basil leaves, coarsely chopped

Heat oil in a wok or pan over high heat and stir-fry garlic and onion about 30 seconds. Add the chile sauce and sugar and stir into a smooth paste. Add the broth or water, bring to a boil, then add soy sauce and tamarind water or lime juice; simmer 1 minute. (The soup can be made in advance up to this point.)

Bring the soup back to a rolling boil and add tofu, bok choy, bean sprouts and tomatoes. Cook about 2 minutes. Adjust seasoning and serve the soup piping hot, garnished with chopped basil leaves.

Makes 4-6 servings.

VERMICELLI & MUSHROOM SOUP

1 tablespoon vegetable oil
½ teaspoon minced garlic
½ teaspoon finely chopped ginger root
1 tablespoon chopped green onion
4½ cups vegetarian broth or water
2 tablespoons soy sauce
1 tablespoon sugar
2 oz. dried bean curd skins, soaked then cut into
    small pieces
2 oz. bean thread vermicelli, soaked then cut into
    short lengths
8-10 Chinese dried mushrooms, soaked and sliced
Salt and freshly ground black pepper
Cilantro leaves, to garnish

Heat oil in a wok or pan over high heat and stir-fry garlic, ginger and green onions 20 seconds, or until fragrant. Add the broth or water and bring to a rolling boil. Add the soy sauce and sugar and simmer about 30 seconds. (The soup can be made in advance up to this point, then brought back to a boil).

Add the bean curd skins, vermicelli and mushrooms and cook 2-3 minutes. Adjust the seasoning and serve garnished with cilantro leaves.

Makes 4-6 servings.

Variation: For nonvegetarians, add 1-2 tablespoons dried shrimp, soaked, if desired. Chicken or meat broth can be used instead of vegetable broth.

—————BARBECUED SHRIMP———

Vegetable oil for deep-frying
4 oz. rice vermicelli
1 lb. raw unpeeled shrimp
2 teaspoons vegetable oil
2-3 green onions, chopped
2-3 small fresh red chiles, chopped
1 tablespoon roasted peanuts, crushed
Cilantro leaves, to garnish
Spicy Fish Sauce, page 14, to serve

Preheat grill or broiler. Heat oil for deep-frying to 300F (150C). Break the vermicelli into short strands and deep-fry, a handful at a time, 30-35 seconds, or until the strands puff up and turn white.

Remove vermicelli and drain, then place on a warm serving dish or plate. Cook the shrimp on the grill, or under the hot broiler, turning once; large shrimp will take about 6-7 minutes, smaller ones 3-4 minutes to cook. When cooked, arrange them on the bed of crispy rice vermicelli.

Heat the 2 teaspoons oil in a small saucepan until hot, removing from the heat before it starts to smoke, add the green onions and chiles and let stand a few minutes, then pour the mixture all over the shrimp. Garnish with crushed peanuts and cilantro leaves and serve hot with the Spicy Fish Sauce as a dip.

Makes 4 servings.

SPICY CRAB

1 clove garlic, chopped
2 shallots or the white parts of 3-4 green onions, chopped
1 teaspoon chopped ginger root
1 tablespoon chopped lemon grass
2-3 tablespoons vegetable oil
1 teaspoon chile sauce
1 tablespoon sugar
3-4 tablespoons coconut milk
About 2 cups chicken broth
3 tablespoons fish sauce
2 tablespoons lime juice or vinegar
Meat from 1 large or 2 medium cooked crabs, cut into small pieces
Salt and freshly ground black pepper
Cilantro leaves, to garnish

Using a pestle and mortar, pound the garlic, shallots or green onions, ginger, and lemon grass to a fine paste. Heat oil in Dutch oven, add the garlic mixture, chile sauce and sugar and stir-fry about 1 minute. Add the coconut milk, broth, fish sauce and lime juice or vinegar and bring to a boil.

Add the crabmeat and season with salt and pepper. Blend well and cook 3-4 minutes, stirring constantly, then serve hot, garnished with cilantro leaves.

Makes 4 servings.

Note: Uncooked crabs can be used for this dish, but increase the cooking time by about 8-10 minutes.

—SHRIMP WITH LEMON GRASS—

2 cloves garlic, chopped
1 tablespoon chopped cilantro
2 tablespoons chopped lemon grass
½ teaspoon black or white peppercorns
3 tablespoons vegetable oil
12-14 oz. raw peeled shrimp, cut in half lengthwise
   if large
2 shallots or 1 small onion, sliced
2-3 small fresh chiles, seeded and chopped
2-3 tomatoes, cut into wedges
1 tablespoon fish sauce
1 tablespoon oyster sauce
2-3 tablespoons chicken broth or water
Cilantro leaves, to garnish

Using a pestle and mortar, pound the garlic, chopped cilantro, lemon grass and peppercorns to a paste. Heat oil in a wok or frying pan and stir-fry the spicy paste 15-20 seconds until fragrant. Add shrimp, shallots or onion, chiles and tomatoes and stir-fry 2-3 minutes.

Add fish sauce, oyster sauce and broth, bring to a boil and simmer 2-3 minutes. Serve garnished with cilantro leaves.

Makes 4 servings.

CURRIED SHRIMP

2 tablespoons vegetable oil
1 teaspoon chopped garlic
2 shallots, or 1 small onion, chopped
2-3 tablespoons mild curry powder
1 cup Vietnamese Hot Sauce, page 17
1 cup chicken broth or water
1 cup coconut milk
10 oz. red potatoes, cut into chunks
2-3 carrots, sliced
3-4 bay leaves
2 tablespoons fish sauce
10 oz. raw peeled shrimp
½ teaspoon salt
1 teaspoon sugar
Cilantro leaves, to garnish

Heat oil in a pan or pot over high heat and stir-fry garlic and shallots or onion about 30 seconds. Blend in the curry powder and cook 30 seconds or until fragrant. Add Vietnamese Hot Sauce, broth or water and coconut milk then bring to a boil, stirring constantly. Add the potatoes, carrots, bay leaves and fish sauce. Reduce heat, cover and simmer 25-30 minutes.

Add shrimp, salt and sugar, then increase the heat and cook 5-6 minutes, stirring constantly. Serve at once, garnished with cilantro leaves.

Makes 4 servings.

──────STIR-FRIED SHRIMP──────

10 oz. raw peeled shrimp
3 tablespoons vegetable oil
1 teaspoon chopped garlic
½ teaspoon chopped ginger root
1 tablespoon chopped green onion
4 oz. straw mushrooms, halved lengthwise
2 oz. water chestnuts, sliced
3 tablespoons fish sauce
1 tablespoon sugar
About 2-3 tablespoons chicken broth or water
1 teaspoon chile sauce (optional)
Salt and freshly ground black pepper
Cilantro leaves, to garnish

Halve shrimp lengthwise. Heat oil in a wok or pan over high heat and stir-fry the garlic, ginger and green onion about 20 seconds. Add the shrimp, mushrooms and water chestnuts and stir-fry about 2 minutes.

Add fish sauce and sugar, stir a few times, then add broth or water. bring to a boil and stir 1 minute. Finally, add the chile sauce, if using, and season with salt and pepper. Garnish with cilantro leaves and serve at once.

Makes 4 servings.

Variation: This is a standard stir-fry recipe. If preferred, use different types of fish or meat, cut into small, thin slices, and cook with any other kind of vegetables.

—SCALLOPS WITH VEGETABLES—

3 tablespoons vegetable oil
1 teaspoon chopped garlic
1-2 small red chiles, seeded and chopped
2 shallots or 1 small onion, chopped
2 oz. snow peas
1 small carrot, thinly sliced
8 oz. fresh scallops, sliced
2 oz. sliced bamboo shoots
2 tablespoons black fungus, soaked and sliced
2-3 green onions, cut into short sections
2 tablespoons fish sauce
1 teaspoon sugar
About 2-3 tablespoons chicken broth or water
1 tablespoon oyster sauce
Salt and freshly ground black pepper
Cilantro leaves, to garnish

Heat oil in a wok or pan over high heat and stir-fry garlic, chiles and shallots or onion for about 20 seconds. Add the snow peas and carrot and stir-fry about 2 minutes. Add scallops, bamboo shoots, fungus and green onions and stir-fry 1 minute.

Add fish sauce and sugar, blend well and stir 1 minute, then add the broth or water. Bring to a boil and stir a few more seconds. Add oyster sauce and season with salt and pepper. Garnish with cilantro leaves and serve at once.

Makes 4 servings.

─────────MIXED SEAFOOD─────────

3 tablespoons vegetable oil
1 teaspoon minced garlic
2 shallots, chopped
4 oz. fish fillet, cut into bite-size pieces
4 oz. squid, prepared as for Squid with Spicy Chiles,
    page 27
4 oz. raw peeled shrimp
4 oz. fresh scallops
4 oz. crabmeat
4 tablespoons Sweet & Sour Sauce, page 16, or
    Vietnamese Hot Sauce, page 17
3 tablespoons fish sauce
3-4 tablespoons chicken broth or water
2 green onions, thinly sliced
Freshly ground black pepper

Heat the oil in a Dutch oven over high heat
and stir-fry the garlic and shallots about 1
minute, or until fragrant. Add the seafood
and stir-fry very gently so that the fish fillet
does not break up. Cook 2-3 minutes, then
add the Sweet and Sour Sauce or
Vietnamese Hot Sauce and the fish sauce
with the broth or water. Stir well and bring
to a boil.

Cover and simmer 3-4 minutes, then
remove the lid and turn off the heat.
Garnish with green onions and pepper and
serve hot straight from the pot.

Makes 4 servings.

Variation: It is not essential to use so many
types of seafood for this dish; if preferred, use
any combination of 2 or 3 types.

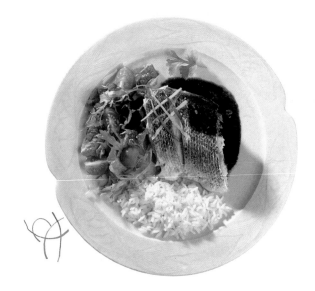

—STEAMED FISH—

1 whole fish, such as sea bass or grouper, weighing
   about 2 lbs., cleaned and scored on both sides at
   1-inch intervals
Salt and freshly ground black pepper
1 teaspoon sugar
1 teaspoon chopped ginger root
1 tablespoon each chopped white and green parts of
   green onion
1 tablespoon fish sauce
2 teaspoons sesame oil
1 tablespoon shredded ginger root
1 tablespoon vegetable oil
1 tablespoon each black bean sauce and soy sauce
2 small fresh red chiles, seeded and shredded
Cilantro leaves, to garnish

Rub the fish inside and out with salt and
pepper, then marinate in a shallow dish with
the sugar, ginger, white parts of green onion,
the fish sauce and sesame oil 30 minutes.
Place fish with marinade in a bowl in a
steamer, or on a rack inside a wok over boiling water, cover and steam 15-20 minutes.

Remove dish from the steamer or wok, place
the ginger and green part of green onion on
top of the fish. Heat vegetable oil in a small
saucepan, add black bean sauce, soy sauce
and chiles and stir-fry 30 seconds, then driz-
zle it over fish. Garnish with cilantro and
serve with rice and a salad.

Makes 4 servings.

Note: If the fish is too big to fit into your
steamer or wok, cut it in half crosswise and
re-assemble it on a warmed plate to serve.

GRILLED FLAT FISH

1¼ lbs. flat fish, such as flounder, cleaned
Salt and freshly ground black pepper
1 tablespoon vegetable oil, plus extra for brushing
½ teaspoon minced garlic
½ teaspoon chopped ginger root
2 shallots, finely chopped
2-3 small fresh red chiles, seeded and chopped
1 tablespoon chopped green onion
2 tablespoons fish sauce and 1 teaspoon sugar
1 tablespoon tamarind water or lime juice
2-3 tablespoons chicken broth or water
2 teaspoons cornstarch

Score both sides of the fish at 1-inch intervals and rub with salt and pepper.

Let fish stand 25 minutes. Meanwhile, preheat broiler. Brush both sides of fish with oil
and broil under the hot broiler about 4 minutes each side until lightly brown but not
burned. Place on a warmed serving dish.

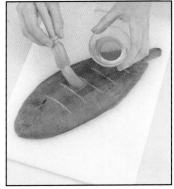

Heat the 1 tablespoon oil in a small pan and
stir-fry the garlic, ginger, shallots, chiles and
green onion 1 minute, then add the fish
sauce, sugar, tamarind water or lime juice
and broth or water. bring to a boil and simmer 30 seconds. Mix cornstarch with
1 tablespoon water and stir into sauce to
thicken. Pour the sauce over the fish. Serve
with carrots and snow peas, garnished with
cilantro leaves.

*Makes 2 servings on its own, or 4-6 servings
with other dishes as part of a meal.*

─────SWEET & SOUR FISH─────

2 lbs. whole fish, such as sea bass, cleaned
Salt and freshly ground black pepper
Vegetable oil for deep-frying
About 2 tablespoons all-purpose flour
1 small onion, shredded
1 small carrot, thinly shredded
1 small green bell pepper, thinly shredded
2 tomatoes, cut into small wedges
2 tablespoons fish sauce
1 cup Sweet & Sour Sauce, page 16
About ½ cup chicken broth or water
1 teaspoon sesame oil (optional)
Cilantro leaves, to garnish

Score both sides of the fish at 1-inch intervals. Rub the fish inside and out with salt and pepper, let stand 15-20 minutes. Heat the oil in a wok or deep-fat fryer to 350F (180C). Coat the fish with flour and deep-fry 3-4 minutes on each side until golden. Remove and drain on paper towels, then place the fish on a warmed serving platter.

Pour off all but about 1 tablespoon oil from the wok, add all the shredded vegetables and tomatoes. Stir-fry about 1 minute, then add the fish sauce, Sweet & Sour Sauce and broth or water. Bring to a boil, then add the sesame oil, if using. Pour sauce over the fish, garnish with cilantro and serve with rice vermicelli.

Makes 4 servings.

Variation: Fish fillets or steaks can be cooked in the same way.

FRIED FISH FILLET

1 (1-lb.) firm white fish fillet, such as halibut, cod,
    haddock or monkfish, cut into ¾-inch pieces
Salt and freshly ground black pepper
1 egg, beaten
3 tablespoons all-purpose flour mixed with 2
    tablespoons water
Vegetable oil for deep-frying
Holy basil and cilantro leaves, to garnish
Spicy Fish Sauce, page 14, to serve

In a dish, season the fish with salt and pepper and let stand 25-30 minutes. Make a batter by blending the egg with the flour and water paste.

Heat oil in a wok or deep-fat fryer to 350F (180C). Coat the fish pieces with batter and deep-fry them, in batches, 3-4 minutes until golden. Remove and drain.

Place the fish pieces on a warmed serving dish with the garnishes. Serve at once with the Spicy Fish Sauce as a dip.

Makes 4 servings.

Variation: A whole fish, boned, skinned and coated in batter, can be deep-fried first then cut into bite-sized pieces for serving.

FISH IN CURRY SAUCE

1 (1-lb.) fish fillet or steak, such as halibut, cod,
  or monkfish, cut into bite-size pieces
Freshly ground black pepper
2 tablespoons fish sauce
1 tablespoon sugar
1 tablespoon vegetable oil
1 clove garlic, finely chopped
2-3 shallots, finely chopped
2-3 tablespoons mild curry powder
1 cup Vietnamese Hot Sauce, page 17
1½ cups chicken broth or water
1 (8-oz.) cake tofu, cut into small cubes
½ teaspoon salt
2-3 green onions, cut into short lengths, to garnish
1-2 small red chiles, seeded and chopped (optional)

In a dish, marinate fish pieces with pepper,
fish sauce and sugar 15-20 minutes. Heat the
oil in a saucepan and stir-fry the garlic and
shallots about 1 minute. Add curry powder
and hot sauce and cook 1 minute, stirring
constantly. Add the broth or water, blend
well and bring to a boil.

Add the fish, tofu pieces and salt, stir very
gently, then reduce heat, cover and simmer
10 minutes. Serve hot, garnished with green
onions and chiles, if using.

Makes 4 servings.

STUFFED SQUID

1 oz. bean thread vermicelli, soaked then cut into
   short strands
½ oz. black fungus, soaked then shredded
8 oz. ground lean pork
Salt and freshly ground black pepper
2 green onions, finely chopped
1 tablespoon fish sauce
1 egg, beaten
8-12 small squid, headless, ready to cook
1-2 tablespoons vegetable oil
Lettuce leaves
Spicy Fish Sauce, page 14, as a dip

In a bowl, mix vermicelli, fungus, pork, salt,
pepper, green onions, fish sauce and egg.

Clean the squid and dry well. Fill the squid
with the stuffing mixture, then cook them
25-30 minutes in a steamer over boiling
water.

Remove the squid from the steamer. Heat
the oil in a frying pan and fry the stuffed
squid 3-4 minutes, turning once. Serve hot
on a bed of lettuce leaves with the Spicy
Fish Sauce as a dip.

Makes 4-6 servings.

Note: Squid are sometimes available already
cleaned, with tentacles still attached. if
desired, the squid can be steamed in
advance, refrigerated, and then fried just
before serving.

STIR-FRIED SQUID

10 oz. squid, prepared as Squid with Spicy Chiles,
   page 27
Salt and freshly ground black pepper
½ cucumber
2 tablespoons vegetable oil
1 clove garlic, finely chopped
1-2 small fresh red chiles, seeded and chopped
1 tablespoon chopped green onion
1 red bell pepper, cut into cubes
2 tablespoons fish sauce or oyster sauce
½ teaspoon sesame oil
Cilantro leaves, to garnish

Cook the squid pieces in boiling water 30
seconds only.

Remove from pan and rinse in cold water,
then drain well. Season with salt and pepper
and let stand 10-15 minutes. Cut the
cucumber in half lengthwise, then across
into 1-inch pieces. Heat oil in a wok or pan
over high heat and stir-fry the garlic, chiles,
and green onion 30 seconds. Add bell pepper cubes, cucumber pieces and squid and
stir-fry 1-2 minutes.

Add the fish or oyster sauce, blend well and
cook 1 minute. Blend in the sesame oil.
Garnish with cilantro leaves and serve with
rice.

Makes 4 servings.

Note: If the food starts to get too dry during
cooking, add about 2-3 tablespoons broth or
water to prevent it burning.

-CHICKEN WITH LEMON GRASS-

1 lb. boned and skinned chicken breast, cut into
   bite-size slices or cubes
Salt and freshly ground black pepper
1 teaspoon minced garlic
2 tablespoons finely chopped lemon grass
1 tablespoon sugar
1 teaspoon chile sauce
3 tablespoons fish sauce
2-3 tablespoons vegetable oil
1 small onion, sliced
1-2 small red chiles, seeded and chopped

Mix chicken with salt, pepper, garlic, lemon grass, sugar, chile sauce and 1 tablespoon fish sauce and marinate 30 minutes.

Heat oil in a wok or frying-pan over high heat and stir-fry onion slices about 1 minute or until opaque. Add chicken pieces, stir to separate them, then add the remaining 2 tablespoons fish sauce and cook 2-3 minutes until the color of chicken changes to white.

Add ¼ cup water to marinade bowl to rinse out, then add to the chicken. bring to a boil and cook 1 minute. Garnish with the chopped chiles and serve with rice noodles.

Makes 4 servings.

Variations: Firm white fish, pork or cubes of tofu can be cooked by the same method. Chicken broth can be used to rinse out the marinade bowl instead of water.

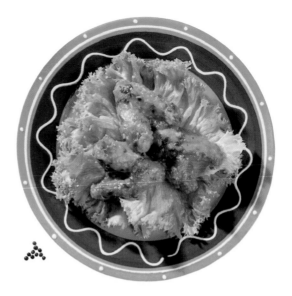

CHICKEN WINGS IN SPICY SAUCE

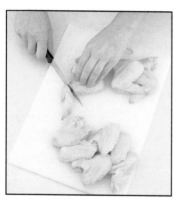

8-12 chicken wings
Salt and freshly ground black pepper
1 tablespoon sugar
1 tablespoon fish sauce
Oil for deep-frying
1 cup Vietnamese Hot Sauce, page 17
About ⅓ cup chicken broth or water
1 tablespoon clear honey
Lettuce leaves

Trim off tip of each chicken wing (these are known as pinions), which can be used for broth making.

In a bowl, marinate the chicken wings with salt, pepper, sugar and fish sauce at least 30 minutes, longer if possible. Heat oil in a wok or deep-fat fryer to 325F (160C) and deep-fry the chicken wings 2-3 minutes until golden; remove and drain on paper towels.

Heat Vietnamese Hot Sauce with chicken broth or water in a saucepan and add the chicken wings. Bring to a boil, reduce heat and simmer 5-6 minutes, stirring constantly, until the sauce is sticky. Add the honey and blend well. Serve hot or cold on a bed of lettuce leaves.

Makes 4-6 servings.

–CHICKEN & COCONUT CURRY–

1 (2¼-lb.) chicken, cut into 10-12 pieces
Salt and freshly ground black pepper
1 teaspoon sugar
1 tablespoon curry powder
3-4 tablespoons vegetable oil
3 red or white potatoes, peeled and cut into cubes
1 teaspoon chopped garlic
1 tablespoon chopped lemon grass
1 onion, cut into small pieces
1 cup Vietnamese Hot Sauce, page 17
2 cups chicken broth or water
2 cups coconut milk
3 bay leaves and 1 carrot, sliced
2 tablespoons fish sauce
Cilantro leaves, to garnish

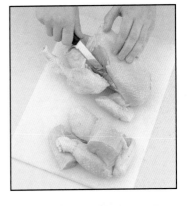

In a dish, marinate the chicken pieces with salt, pepper, sugar, and curry powder in the refrigerator at least 1 hour. Heat oil in a large pan and fry the potatoes 3-4 minutes until brown – it is not necessary to completely cook the potatoes at this stage. Remove potatoes from pan and set aside.

In the same oil, stir-fry garlic, lemon grass and onion about 30 seconds. Add the chicken pieces and stir-fry 2-3 minutes, then add Vietnamese Hot Sauce, broth or water, coconut milk and bay leaves. bring to a boil, and add the browned potatoes, carrot slices and fish sauce. Blend well, then cover and simmer 15-20 minutes, stirring occasionally to make sure nothing is stuck on the bottom of the pan. Garnish with cilantro leaves and serve.

Makes 4-6 servings.

GRILLED CHICKEN DRUMSTICKS

1-2 cloves garlic, chopped
1-2 stalks lemon grass, chopped
2 shallots, chopped
1-2 small red or green chiles, chopped
1 tablespoon chopped cilantro
¼ cup fish sauce
6-8 chicken drumsticks, skinned
Lettuce leaves
Spicy Fish Sauce, page 14, to serve

Using a pestle and mortar, pound garlic, lemon grass, shallots, chiles and cilantro to a paste.

In a medium bowl, thoroughly blend pounded mixture with the fish sauce to a smooth paste. Add drumsticks and coat well with the paste. Cover the bowl and leave to marinate 2-3 hours in the refrigerator, turning drumsticks every 30 minutes or so.

Preheat grill or broiler. Cook the drumsticks over grill or under the broiler 10-15 minutes, turning frequently and basting with the marinade remaining in the bowl the first 5 minutes only. Serve hot on a bed of lettuce leaves with the Spicy Fish Sauce as a dip.

Makes 4-6 servings.

————STIR-FRIED CHICKEN————

8 oz. boned and skinned chicken breasts
2 teaspoons cornstarch
2 teaspoons fish sauce
Salt and freshly ground pepper
2-3 tablespoons vegetable oil
½ teaspoon minced garlic
1 teaspoon finely chopped lemon grass
1 teaspoon chopped ginger root
4-6 dried small red chiles
2 oz. snow peas, trimmed
½ red bell pepper, cut into cubes
2 oz. sliced bamboo shoots, drained
1 teaspoon sugar
1 tablespoon rice vinegar
2 tablespoons oyster sauce
½ teaspoon sesame oil

Cut chicken into bite-size slices or cubes. Mix cornstarch with 1 tablespoon water. Place chicken in a bowl with cornstarch paste and fish sauce. Season with salt and pepper and marinate 20-25 minutes. Heat oil in a wok or frying pan and stir-fry the garlic, lemon grass, ginger and chiles 30 seconds. Add the chicken pieces and stir-fry about 1 minute until the color of the chicken changes to white.

Add vegetables and cook 2-3 minutes, stirring constantly, then add sugar, vinegar, oyster sauce and 3-4 tablespoons water. Blend well, bring to a boil and add the sesame oil. Serve at once with flat rice noodles.

Makes 4 servings.

Variation: Use chicken broth instead of the 3-4 tablespoons water.

CHICKEN HOT POT

1 lb. chicken thigh meat, boned and cut into small
  bite-size pieces
Salt and freshly ground pepper
2 teaspoons sugar
1 tablespoon each lime juice and fish sauce
1 tablespoon vegetable oil
2 cloves garlic, sliced, and 2 shallots, chopped
1 tablespoon dried small red chiles
2 tablespoons crushed yellow bean sauce
About 2 cups chicken broth
2 green onions, cut into short sections
Cilantro leaves, to garnish

Marinate the chicken with salt, pepper,
sugar, lime juice and fish sauce 1-2 hours.

Heat the oil in a Dutch oven over high heat
and stir-fry garlic, shallots and chiles about 1
minute, then add yellow bean sauce and stir
until combined.

Add the chicken pieces and stir-fry 1-2 minutes. Add chicken broth, blend well and
bring to a boil, then reduce heat, cover and
simmer 15-20 minutes. Uncover and stir in
green onions. Garnish with cilantro and
serve straight from the pot. Serve with rice.

Makes 4 servings.

Note: The longer the chicken is marinated,
the better the flavor; marinate up to 2 hours
in the refrigerator.

GRILLED QUAIL

4 cleaned quail, each split down the backbone and
  pressed flat
Salt and freshly ground black pepper
1 teaspoon minced garlic
1 tablespoon finely chopped lemon grass
1 teaspoon sugar
1 tablespoon fish sauce
1 tablespoon lime juice or vinegar
1-2 tablespoons vegetable oil
Lettuce leaves
Cilantro leaves, to garnish
Spicy Fish Sauce, page 14, to serve

Rub the 4 quail all over with plenty of salt
and pepper.

In a medium bowl, blend garlic, lemon grass,
sugar, fish sauce and lime juice or vinegar.
Add quail, turning to coat in the mixture,
then marinate 2-3 hours in the refrigerator,
turning over occasionally.

Preheat grill or broiler. Brush quail with oil
and cook over grill or under broiler 6-8 minutes each side, basting with remaining marinade during first 5 minutes of cooking. Serve
quail on a bed of lettuce leaves, garnished
with cilantro leaves, accompanied by Spicy
Fish Sauce as a dip.

Makes 4 servings.

AROMATIC DUCK

2 half or 4 quarter portions of duck (2 breasts and
   2 legs)
Salt and freshly ground black pepper
1 tablespoon five-spice powder
4-5 small pieces ginger root
3-4 green onions, cut into short sections
3-4 tablespoons Chinese rice wine or dry sherry
12 sheets dried rice paper, halved if large
Fresh mint, basil and cilantro leaves
Spicy Fish Sauce, page 14

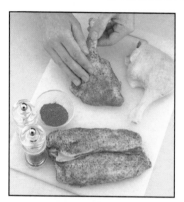

Rub the salt, pepper and five-spice powder
all over the duck portions.

In a shallow dish, mix ginger, green onions
and rice wine or sherry, add duck portions
and marinate at least 3-4 hours in the refrigerator, turning the duck pieces occasionally.
Steam the duck portions with marinade in a
dish in a steamer 2-3 hours. Remove the
duck portions from the liquid. (The duck
can be cooked up to this stage in advance, if
desired.)

Preheat oven to 450F (230C) and bake the
duck pieces, skin-side up, 10-15 minutes,
then pull the meat off the bone. Meanwhile,
soften dried rice paper in warm water. Place
about 2 tablespoons of meat in each half
sheet of rice paper, add a few mint, basil and
cilantro leaves, roll into a neat bundle, then
dip the roll in the Spicy Fish Sauce before
eating it.

Makes 4-6 servings.

——VIETNAMESE ROAST DUCK——

1 teaspoon minced garlic
2-3 shallots, finely chopped
2 teaspoons five-spice powder
2 tablespoons sugar
¼ cup red rice vinegar
1 tablespoon fish sauce
1 tablespoon soy sauce
4 quarter portions duck (2 breasts and 2 legs)
1 cup coconut milk
Salt and freshly ground black pepper
Watercress, to serve
Cilantro leaves, to garnish

In a bowl, mix garlic, shallots, five-spice powder, sugar, vinegar, fish and soy sauces.

Add duck pieces and marinate at least 2-3 hours or overnight in the refrigerator, turning occasionally. Preheat oven to 425F (220C). Remove duck portions from marinade and place, skin-side up, on a rack in a baking pan and cook in the oven 45 minutes, without turning or basting.

Remove duck and keep warm. Remove fat from the drip pan. Heat the marinade in the baking pan, add the coconut milk, bring to a boil and simmer 5 minutes. Season with salt and pepper, then pour sauce into a serving bowl. Serve duck portions on a bed of watercress, garnished with cilantro leaves.

Makes 4-6 servings.

Note: The duck portions can be chopped through the bone into bite-size pieces serving, if desired.

-DUCK BREASTS IN SPICY SAUCE-

2 pairs of duck breasts, boned but not skinned
Salt and freshly ground black pepper
1 teaspoon chopped garlic
2 shallots or 1 small onion, finely chopped
1 tablespoon chopped lemon grass
1 tablespoon chopped ginger root
2-3 tablespoons vegetable oil
1 teaspoon sugar
2 tablespoons fish sauce
1 teaspoon chile sauce
½ cup chicken broth or water
2 teaspoons cornstarch
½ teaspoon sesame oil
1-2 small red chiles, seeded and shredded
Cilantro leaves, to garnish

Make a few shallow crisscross cuts on the skin side of the duck breasts. Rub with the salt and pepper and let stand 15-20 minutes. Meanwhile, using a pestle and mortar, pound garlic, shallots or onion, lemon grass and ginger to a paste.

Heat oil in a wok or pan and fry duck pieces, skin-side down, 2-3 minutes, then turn pieces over and cook 2 minutes. Add garlic mixture and stir to coat well, then add sugar, fish and chile sauces. Cook, stirring, 1 minute. Add broth or water, bring to a boil and cook 5-6 minutes, stirring. Mix cornstarch with 1 tablespoon water and stir into the sauce. Blend in sesame oil. Slice duck, garnish with chiles and cilantro and serve with rice vermicelli.

Makes 4-6 servings.

—SPICY PORK & LEMON GRASS—

1 clove garlic, chopped
2 shallots, chopped
3 tablespoons chopped lemon grass
1 tablespoon sugar
1 tablespoon fish sauce
Salt and freshly ground black pepper
12 oz. pork fillet, cut into small, thin slices
2-3 tablespoons vegetable oil
2-3 stalks celery, thinly sliced
4 oz. straw mushrooms, halved lengthwise
4 small red chiles, seeded and shredded
2 green onions, shredded
1 tablespoon soy sauce
About ¼ cup chicken broth or water
2 teaspoons cornstarch
Cilantro leaves, to garnish

Using a pestle and mortar, pound the garlic, shallots and lemon grass to a paste. Transfer to a medium bowl and add the sugar, fish sauce, salt and pepper. Blend well, then add the pork slices, turning to coat them with the mixture, and marinate 25-30 minutes.

Heat oil in a wok or frying-pan and stir-fry pork slices 2 minutes. Add the celery, straw mushrooms, chiles, green onions and soy sauce and stir-fry 2-3 minutes. Use the broth to rinse out the marinade bowl and add to the pork. bring to a boil. Mix cornstarch with 1 tablespoon water and add to sauce. Cook, stirring, until thickened. Garnish with cilantro and serve at once with a mixture of rice and wild rice.

Makes 4 servings.

SPICY PORK HOT POT

1 tablespoon vegetable oil
2 cloves garlic, chopped
2 shallots, chopped
1 lb. lean pork, cut into bite-size pieces
3 tablespoons sugar
3 tablespoons fish sauce
1 teaspoon five-spice powder
About 1 cup chicken broth or water
Salt and freshly ground black pepper
2-3 green onions, cut into short sections, to garnish

Heat oil in a Dutch oven and stir-fry the garlic and shallots about 1 minute or until fragrant.

Add the pork pieces and stir-fry them about 2 minutes, or until the pork turns almost white in color.

Add sugar, fish sauce and five-spice powder, stir 1 minute, then add broth or water. bring to a boil, reduce heat, cover and simmer 15-20 minutes. Adjust seasoning, garnish with green onions and serve with snow peas and bell peppers.

Makes 4 servings.

Variation: Chicken, lamb, veal or beef can all be cooked in the same way; increase the cooking time by 10-15 minutes for lamb and veal, 20-25 minutes for beef.

——————STIR-FRIED PORK——————

1 teaspoon minced garlic
2 shallots, finely chopped
½ teaspoon chopped ginger root
1 teaspoon sugar
1 tablespoon fish sauce
Salt and freshly ground black pepper
1 lb. pork fillet, cut into small slices or cubes
2-3 tablespoons vegetable oil
4 oz. sliced bamboo shoots, drained
2 small red chiles, seeded and chopped
2 green onions, chopped
2 tablespoons oyster sauce
About ¼ cup chicken broth or water
2 teaspoons cornstarch
½ teaspoon sesame oil
Cilantro leaves, to garnish

In a bowl, mix garlic, shallots, ginger, sugar, fish sauce, salt and pepper. Add pork and marinate 25-30 minutes.

Heat oil in a wok or frying-pan over high heat and stir-fry pork pieces 2 minutes, then add bamboo shoots, chiles, green onions and oyster sauce and stir-fry 4-5 minutes. Rinse out the marinade bowl with the broth or water and add to the pork mixture. Bring to a boil. Mix cornstarch with 1 tablespoon water and stir into sauce. Cook, stirring, until thickened. Add sesame oil, garnish with cilantro leaves and serve with halved cucumber slices.

Makes 4 servings.

——PORK WITH VEGETABLES——

8 oz. pork fillet, thinly shredded
Salt and freshly ground black pepper
3 tablespoons vegetable oil
2 shallots, finely chopped
1 teaspoon chopped ginger root
8 oz. bean sprouts
1 small red bell pepper, cored and thinly sliced
2-3 green onions, shredded
2 tablespoons soy sauce
Cilantro leaves, to garnish

In a bowl, season the pork with salt and pepper; let stand 10-15 minutes.

Heat oil in a wok or frying pan over high heat and stir-fry the shallots and ginger about 1 minute. Add the pork and stir-fry 2-3 minutes, until the shreds are separated and the pork turns almost white in color.

Add bean sprouts, red bell pepper, green onions and soy sauce and stir-fry a further 2-3 minutes. Garnish with cilantro and serve at once.

Makes 4 servings.

—VIETNAMESE BEEF PARCELS—

2 cloves garlic, chopped
3 shallots, chopped
2 tablespoons chopped lemon grass
1 tablespoon sugar
1 tablespoon fish sauce
1 tablespoon sesame oil
½ teaspoon freshly ground black pepper
1 lb. beef fillet, cut across the grain into thin slices
    about 2 inches long
8 sheets dried rice paper, halved if large
Mint and cilantro leaves
Spicy Fish Sauce, page 14

Using a pestle and mortar, pound the garlic, shallots, lemon grass and sugar to a paste.

Place paste in a medium bowl with fish sauce, sesame oil and pepper. Blend well. Add beef and marinate 1 hour, or longer in the refrigerator. Meanwhile, preheat the grill or broiler, or preheat oven to 450F (230C). Cook beef on grill 1 minute, under broiler 2-3 minutes, or in oven 6-8 minutes, turning once.

To serve, dip each piece of dried rice paper in warm water to soften it, then place a slice of beef on one end of the paper, put a mint leaf and some cilantro on top of the beef and roll into a neat parcel. Dip the parcels in the Spicy Fish Sauce before eating.

Makes 4 servings.

Note: This dish can also be served as a starter, in which case it will make 6-8 servings.

─── STIR-FRIED BEEF STEAK ───

8 oz. beef steak, cut into small, thin slices, about
   1 inch square
¼ teaspoon freshly ground black pepper
1 teaspoon sugar
1 tablespoon fish sauce
2 tablespoons vegetable oil
1 clove garlic, chopped
1 small onion, sliced
1 green bell pepper, cut into cubes
4 oz. sliced bamboo shoots, drained
1 firm tomato, cut into 8 wedges
2 green onions, cut into short lengths
2 tablespoons soy or oyster sauce
2 teaspoons cornstarch

Mix beef with black pepper, sugar and fish sauce and marinate 15-20 minutes. Heat oil in a wok or frying pan over high heat and stir-fry garlic and onion about 1 minute. Add the beef and stir-fry 1 minute.

Add the bell pepper, bamboo shoots, tomato and green onions. Stir-fry 2-3 minutes, then blend in the soy or oyster sauce. Mix the cornstarch with 1 tablespoon water and stir into mixture. Cook, stirring, until thickened. Serve with rice noodles.

Makes 4 servings.

SPICY BEEF STEW

1 tablespoon vegetable oil
2 cloves garlic, chopped
1 onion, chopped
1 stalk lemon grass, chopped
1 lb. stew beef, cut into bite-size cubes
2½ cups beef stock or water
5-6 tablespoons soy or fish sauce
1 teaspoon chile sauce
2 teaspoons five-spice powder
1 tablespoon sugar
2-3 green onions, chopped
Freshly ground black pepper
Cilantro leaves, to garnish

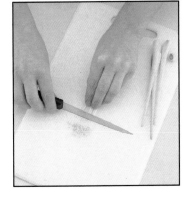

Heat oil in a Dutch oven over high heat and stir-fry garlic, onion, and lemon grass about 1 minute. Add the beef and stir-fry 2-3 minutes, or until the color of the meat changes. Add the stock or water, bring to a boil, then add the soy or fish sauce, chile sauce, five-spice powder and sugar. Blend well, then reduce heat, cover and simmer 45-50 minutes.

Add green onions, season with pepper and cook 5 minutes. Garnish with cilantro leaves and serve straight from the pot, accompanied by carrots and baby corn.

Makes 4 servings.

Variation: Substitute curry powder the five-spice powder to make beef curry.

——BEEF & SEAFOOD FONDUE——

8 oz. beef fillet, sliced paper thin
4 oz. firm white fish fillet, thinly sliced
4 oz. cleaned squid, prepared as Squid with Spicy
   Chiles, page 27
6 raw peeled shrimp, cut in half lengthwise
1 tomato and 1 onion, thinly sliced
Freshly ground black pepper
1 tablespoon sesame oil
2 teaspoons vegetable oil
1 clove garlic, chopped
2 shallots, chopped
1 tablespoon each tomato paste and sugar
1 teaspoon salt
2 tablespoons rice vinegar
3 cups beef stock or water

Arrange the beef and seafood on a platter in separate sections. Place tomato and onion slices in the center and sprinkle pepper and sesame oil all over them. Set aside while you prepare the broth.

Heat vegetable oil in a saucepan over high heat and stir-fry the garlic and shallots about 30 seconds, then add the tomato paste, sugar, salt and rice vinegar. Blend well, then add the broth or water, bring to a boil and transfer to a Chinese hot pot or fondue.

FONDUE ACCOMPANIMENTS

2 oz. bean thread vermicelli, soaked then cut into
    short lengths
6-8 Chinese dried mushrooms, soaked and each
    cut in half or quartered
2 (8-oz.) cakes tofu, cut into small cubes
4 oz. bok choy (Chinese cabbage), cut into small
    pieces
Dried rice paper or lettuce leaves
Mint and cilantro leaves
Spicy Fish Sauce, page 14

Arrange the vermicelli, mushrooms, tofu
cubes and bok choy on a serving platter in
separate sections.

If using large sheets of rice paper, cut in half;
if using lettuce leaves, separate them, and
place on a serving dish. Place spicy sauce in
individual small saucers for dipping. To
serve, bring boiling broth in the hot pot or
fondue to the table; each person picks up a
slice of beef or some seafood with vegetables
and dips them into the broth to be cooked
very briefly – usually no more than 1 minute.

Meanwhile, dip a piece of rice paper in hot
water to soften it. Quickly remove the food
from the broth and place in the middle of
the rice paper or a lettuce leaf, add a few
mint and cilantro leaves, then fold over to
make into a neat parcel. Dip the parcel in
the Spicy Fish Sauce before eating.

Makes 4-6 servings.

LAMB WITH SPICY HOT SAUCE

10 oz. lamb steak, thinly sliced
Salt and freshly ground black pepper
1 teaspoon minced garlic
1 teaspoon chopped ginger root
1 tablespoon fish sauce
3 tablespoons vegetable oil
8 oz. spinach or any green vegetable
1 tablespoon oyster sauce
2-3 tablespoons Vietnamese Hot Sauce, page 17
About 2-3 tablespoons stock or water
½ teaspoon sesame oil
Mint sprigs, to garnish

Marinate lamb with salt, pepper, garlic, ginger, and fish sauce in refrigerator 2-3 hours.

Heat about half of the oil in a wok or pan over high heat and stir-fry the spinach or green vegetable about 2 minutes. Blend in the oyster sauce, then place on a warmed serving dish.

Wipe clean the wok or pan and add the remaining oil. When hot, add the lamb slices and Vietnamese Hot Sauce and stir-fry 2 minutes. Rinse out remaining marinade with stock or water and add to the lamb. Bring to a boil and cook 2-3 minutes, stirring all the time. Add the sesame oil, then spoon the lamb over the spinach or green vegetable. Garnish with mint and serve at once.

Makes 4 servings.

—VEGETABLES IN SPICY SAUCE—

2-3 tablespoons vegetable oil
1 (8-oz.) cake tofu, cut into small cubes
½ teaspoon minced garlic
2 shallots, sliced
1 tablespoon curry powder
2 tablespoons soy sauce
1 tablespoon chopped lemon grass
1 tablespoon chopped ginger root
1 teaspoon chile sauce (optional)
1 cup coconut milk
½ teaspoon salt
1 tablespoon sugar
2 small carrots and 1 onion, sliced
4-6 oz. cauliflower flowerets
8 oz. green beans, trimmed and cut in half
2 firm tomatoes, cut into wedges

Heat oil in a wok or large fry-pan and fry the
tofu until browned on all sides. Remove and
drain. Stir-fry the garlic and shallots in the
same oil about 1 minute, then add curry
powder, soy sauce, lemon grass, ginger and
chile sauce, if using, and cook 1 minute.
Add the coconut milk, salt and sugar and
bring to a boil.

Add the carrots, onion, cauliflower, beans
and tofu and stir-fry 3-4 minutes, then add
the tomatoes. Blend well and cook 2 minutes. Serve at once.

Makes 4-6 servings.

Variation: For nonvegetarians, either fish
sauce or oyster sauce can be used instead of
soy sauce this dish.

──STIR-FRIED VEGETABLES──

2 tablespoons vegetable oil
1 clove garlic, chopped
1 teaspoon chopped ginger root
1 carrot, sliced
4 oz. baby corn cobs, halved
1-2 young leeks, sliced
1-2 bok choy (Chinese cabbage), cut into small
   pieces
4 oz. snow peas
4 oz. bean sprouts
Salt and freshly ground black pepper
1 tablespoon soy sauce
2 teaspoons cornstarch
½ teaspoon sesame oil (optional)

Heat oil in a wok or frying-pan over high heat and stir-fry garlic and ginger about 30 seconds. Add the carrot, baby corn, leeks, bok choy and snow peas and stir-fry about 2 minutes.

Add bean sprouts and stir-fry 1 minute. Add salt, pepper and soy sauce and stir-fry 2 minutes. Mix cornstarch with 1 tablespoon water and stir into the gravy. Cook, stirring, until thickened. Finally blend in sesame oil, if using, then serve vegetables hot or cold.

Makes 4-6 servings.

Variation: Fish or oyster sauce can be used instead of soy sauce a nonvegetarians.

——————MIXED VEGETABLES——————

2-3 tablespoons vegetable oil
12 oz. bok choy (Chinese leaves), cut into large
  pieces
4-6 dried Chinese mushrooms, soaked and sliced
2 oz. bean thread vermicelli, soaked and cut into
  short lengths
2 oz. dried bean curd sticks, soaked and cut into
  short sections
2 oz. dried lily buds, soaked
4 oz. sliced bamboo shoots, drained
4 oz. broccoli flowerets
Salt and freshly ground black pepper
2 tablespoons soy sauce
½ teaspoon sesame oil

Heat oil in a Dutch oven over high heat and stir-fry the bok choy 2-3 minutes.

Add the soaked mushrooms, vermicelli, bean curd sticks, lily buds, bamboo shoots and broccoli and stir-fry 2 minutes, then add salt, pepper, soy sauce and some of the mushroom soaking water. bring to a boil, cover and simmer 2-3 minutes. Blend in the sesame oil. Serve hot straight from the pot.

Makes 4-6 servings.

FRIED GREEN BEANS

2 tablespoons vegetable oil
1 clove garlic, chopped
1 small onion, sliced
1 lb. green beans, trimmed and cut in half
About 2 tablespoons stock or water
2-3 small red chiles, seeded and shredded
2 firm tomatoes, cut into wedges
Salt and freshly ground black pepper
½ teaspoon sugar

Heat oil in a wok or frying pan and stir-fry the garlic and onion about 1 minute.

Add the green beans and stir-fry 2-3 minutes, adding a little broth or water if the beans seem to be too dry.

Add chiles and tomatoes, and stir-fry 1 minute, then add salt, pepper and sugar and blend well. Serve the beans hot or cold.

Makes 4 servings.

──ZUCCHINI WITH GINGER──

2 tablespoons vegetable oil
small piece ginger root, peeled and sliced
1 teaspoon minced garlic
1 lb. zucchini, peeled and cut into small wedges
1 small carrot, sliced
2-3 tablespoons stock or water
2 oz. straw mushrooms, halved lengthwise
1 tomato, sliced
2 green onions, cut into short lengths
Salt and freshly ground pepper
½ teaspoon sugar
1 tablespoon fish sauce

Heat oil in a wok or frying pan over high heat and stir-fry ginger and garlic about 30 seconds until fragrant. Add the zucchini and carrot and stir-fry about 2 minutes, then add the broth or water to create steam, and cook, stirring, 1-2 minutes.

Add straw mushrooms, tomato and green onions with salt, pepper and sugar, blend well and cook 1-2 minutes. Sprinkle with fish sauce and serve at once.

Makes 4 servings.

Variation: Other fresh delicate vegetables, such as asparagus, snow peas, green bell peppers or cucumber can all be cooked in the same way.

—EGGPLANT IN SPICY SAUCE—

1 lb. eggplant, cut into small strips
2-3 tablespoons vegetable oil
1 clove garlic, chopped
2 shallots, finely chopped
Salt and freshly ground black pepper
½ teaspoon sugar
2-3 small hot red chiles, seeded and chopped
2 tomatoes, cut into wedges
1 tablespoon soy sauce
1 teaspoon chile sauce
1 tablespoon rice vinegar
About ½ cup vegetarian stock
2 teaspoons cornstarch
½ teaspoon sesame oil
Cilantro leaves, to garnish

Stir-fry the eggplant in a dry wok or frying pan 3-4 minutes or until soft and a small amount of natural juice has appeared. Remove and set aside. Add the oil and heat. Stir-fry garlic and shallots about 30 seconds. Add the eggplant, salt, pepper, sugar and chiles and stir-fry 2-3 minutes.

Add the tomatoes, soy sauce, chile sauce, vinegar and stock, blend well and bring to a boil. Reduce heat and simmer 3-4 minutes. Mix cornstarch with 1 tablespoon water and stir into sauce. Cook, stirring, until thickened. Blend in sesame oil, garnish and serve.

Makes 4 servings.

Variation: For nonvegetarians, fish sauce or shrimp paste can be used instead of soy sauce. Chicken stock can be used instead of the vegetarian stock.

SPICY TOFU

Vegetable oil for deep-frying
2 (8-oz.) cakes tofu, cut into small cubes
1 clove garlic, chopped
2 shallots, chopped
2-3 small red chiles, seeded and chopped
2 leeks, sliced
About ½ oz. black fungus, soaked and cut into small
    pieces
Salt and freshly ground black pepper
½ teaspoon sugar
1 tablespoon rice vinegar
1 tablespoon crushed black bean sauce
About ¼ cup vegetarian stock or water
2 teaspoons cornstarch
½ teaspoon sesame oil
Chopped green onions, to garnish

Heat oil in a wok or deep-fat fryer to 375F
(190C) and deep-fry the tofu cubes until
browned on all sides. Remove and drain.
Pour off the excess oil, leaving about 1 tablespoon in the wok, stir-fry the garlic, shallots,
and chiles about 30 seconds, then add the
leeks and stir-fry 2-3 minutes.

Add tofu, black fungus, salt and pepper. Sir-
fry 1 minute, then blend in sugar, vinegar,
black bean sauce and stock or water. Bring
to a boil and simmer 1-2 minutes. Mix cornstarch with 1 tablespoon water and stir into
mixture. Cook, stirring, until thickened.
Add sesame oil, garnish and serve.

Makes 4 servings.

Note: a nonvegetarian dish, add about 6 oz.
chopped beef with the leeks in step 2, and
increase seasonings by half.

—STEAMED TOFU & FISH SAUCE—

1 tablespoon dried shrimp
2 oz. ground pork
2 tablespoons chopped preserved vegetable
1 tablespoon chopped green onion
Salt and freshly ground black pepper
1 teaspoon sesame oil
1 tablespoon vegetable oil
2 (8-oz.) cakes tofu, each cut into 4 squares
2 tablespoons fish sauce
Cilantro leaves, to garnish

In a bowl, mix the shrimp, pork, preserved vegetable, green onion, salt, pepper and sesame oil. Blend well and set aside.

Grease a heatproof plate with the vegetable oil and place the tofu on it. Pour the fish sauce evenly all over the tofu, then place about 1 tablespoon of the shrimp and pork mixture on top of each square.

Place the plate with the tofu in a steamer over boiling water, cover and cook over high heat 12-15 minutes. Serve at once, garnished with cilantro leaves.

Makes 4 servings.

───────VIETNAMESE SALAD───────

4-6 lettuce leaves
½ cucumber, cut into thin strips lengthwise
1-2 carrots, peeled and cut into thin strips
1 small onion, thinly shredded
2 firm tomatoes, cut into wedges
2-3 small red chiles, seeded and chopped
Mint leaves
Cilantro leaves
Spicy Fish Sauce, page 14, or Vegetarian Dipping
  Sauce, page 15, to serve

Line a serving platter with lettuce leaves.

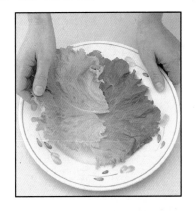

Arrange separate sections of cucumber and carrot strips, shredded onion and tomato wedges on the bed of lettuce leaves.

Arrange separate mounds of chopped red chiles, mint and cilantro leaves on top of the vegetables. Serve with either the Spicy Fish Sauce or Vegetarian Dip Sauce poured over the salad at the table.

Makes 4 servings.

Note: At Vietnamese meals this vegetable platter is served either as a starter or as a side dish, and the vegetables can be varied according to seasonal availablity.

—STEAMED CHICKEN & RICE—

Salt and freshly ground black pepper
1 teaspoon each sugar and sesame oil
1 tablespoon fish sauce
2 teaspoons chopped garlic
10 oz. chicken thigh meat, boned and skinned, cut
  into bite-size pieces
3 tablespoons vegetable oil
4 shallots, finely chopped
2½ cups long grain rice
2 cups chicken broth
8 dried Chinese mushrooms, soaked and cut into
  small pieces
4 oz. canned straw mushrooms, drained
1 tablespoon each soy sauce and oyster sauce
2 green onions, chopped
Cilantro leaves, to garnish

In a bowl, mix salt, pepper, sugar, sesame oil, fish sauce and half the garlic. Add chicken and marinate 25-30 minutes. Heat about 2 tablespoons vegetable oil in a Dutch oven and stir-fry the remaining garlic and half of the chopped shallots about 1 minute. Add the rice and stir-fry about 5 minutes, then add the broth. Stir and bring to a boil, then reduce the heat to very low, cover and cook 8-10 minutes.

Heat remaining oil in a wok or saucepan and stir-fry remaining shallots until opaque. Add chicken pieces and stir-fry 2-3 minutes. Add mushrooms and soy sauce and cook, stirring, about 5 minutes. Uncover the rice and fluff up with a fork. Spoon chicken and mushroom mixture on top of the rice, add oyster sauce and green onions, cover and cook a further 5 minutes. Garnish with cilantro leaves and serve at once.

Makes 4-6 servings.

SEAFOOD FRIED RICE

1 cup long grain rice
3 tablespoons vegetable oil
1 clove garlic, chopped
2 shallots, chopped
4 oz. small cooked peeled shrimp
4 oz. crabmeat, flaked
Salt and freshly ground black pepper
2-3 eggs, beaten
2 tablespoons fish or soy sauce
Chopped green onion, to garnish

The day before, cook the rice as on page 12, then refrigerate it, so that it is cold and dry when required.

Heat about 1 tablespoon oil in a wok or frying-pan over high heat and stir-fry the garlic and shallots about 30 seconds, then add the shrimp and crabmeat with salt and pepper. Stir-fry 2-3 minutes, remove from pan and set aside.

Heat remaining oil in the pan and lightly scramble beaten eggs. When just beginning to set hard, add the rice and stir-fry mixture 2-3 minutes. Add shrimp and crabmeat with the fish or soy sauce and blend well. Garnish with chopped green onion and serve at once.

Makes 4 servings.

—VEGETARIAN FRIED NOODLES—

2 tablespoons vegetable oil
1 clove garlic, chopped
1 onion, sliced
2-3 small red chiles, seeded and shredded
1 carrot, thinly shredded
8 oz. bean sprouts
salt and freshly ground black pepper
8 oz. rice vermicelli, soaked in hot water 5 minutes,
    drained and cut into short lengths
2 tablespoons soy sauce
Shredded green onion, to garnish

Heat oil in a wok or frying pan and stir-fry garlic and onion 1 minute or until softened.

Add the chiles and carrot shreds and cook, stirring, 2 minutes, then add the bean sprouts, salt and pepper. Blend well and stir-fry 2 minutes.

Add the rice vermicelli with the soy sauce, mix and toss, then cook 2-3 minutes. Garnish with shredded green onion and serve at once.

Makes 4 servings.

Note: Serve this dish with chile sauce or Spicy Fish Sauce, page 14, if desired.

———SPICY COLD NOODLES———

3 tablespoons vegetable oil
2 eggs, beaten
1 clove garlic and 2 shallots, chopped
4 oz. pork, shredded
4 oz. peeled raw shrimp
1 tablespoon dried shrimp, soaked
1-2 tablespoons preserved vegetable, chopped
2 oz. bean sprouts
2 small red chiles, seeded and chopped
Salt and freshly ground black pepper
2 tablespoons fish sauce
8 oz. rice vermicelli, cooked in boiling water 5
    minutes, drained and rinsed
3 tablespoons crushed peanuts
2-3 green onions, shredded

Heat about 1 tablespoon oil in a wok or pan and scramble the eggs until just set, then break up into small pieces and remove. Heat the remaining oil and stir-fry the garlic and shallots about 30 seconds. Add the pork and raw shrimp and stir-fry 1-2 minutes. Add the dried shrimp, preserved vegetable, bean sprouts, scrambled eggs, chiles, salt, pepper and fish sauce. Blend well and stir-fry 2-3 minutes. Set aside.

Place the vermicelli on a large serving dish or plate, add the shrimp with a mound of crushed peanuts and green onions on top.

Makes 4 servings.

Note: Serve with chile sauce and/or Spicy Fish Sauce, page 14, if desired.

—BEEF & RICE NOODLE SOUP—

1 (3 lb.) oxtail, cut into pieces
2 stalks lemon grass, chopped
1 large piece ginger root, peeled
1 onion, sliced
5-6 whole star anise
6 cloves
1 cinnamon stick (optional)
1 tablespoon sugar
1 teaspoon salt
2 tablespoons fish sauce
1 lb. flat rice noodles, soaked in hot water 10
   minutes, then drained
8-10 oz. sirloin beef steak, cut into small paper-thin
   slices

Trim off as much excess fat from oxtail as possible. Place pieces in a large pot, add lemon grass, ginger, onion, star anise, cloves, and cinnamon stick, if using. Add 9 cups water and bring to a boil. Reduce heat and simmer oxtail at least 2½ hours, skimming the surface occasionally to remove the scum.

Strain the broth and discard the oxtail and flavoring ingredients (the meat from the bones can be used another dish). Add sugar, salt, and fish sauce to the clear broth, bring back to a boil and simmer 2-3 minutes. (At this stage, the broth can be cooled and refrigerated 1-2 days. The fat can be removed from the top and the broth reheated ready for use.)

SOUP ACCOMPANIMENTS
4 oz. bean sprouts
½ cucumber, thinly shredded
4-5 lettuce leaves, shredded
1 onion, thinly sliced
4 small red chiles, seeded and chopped
2 limes, cut into wedges
Mint, basil and cilantro leaves
Chile sauce

Arrange the accompaniments on a serving platter. Place a portion of the rice noodles in each of 4-6 large individual serving bowls.

Bring the beef broth to a rolling boil. Place a few slices of beef steak on top of noodles and pour in the boiling broth to fill the bowls about three-quarters full. Bring them to the table.

Each person takes a small amount of bean sprouts, cucumber, lettuce, onion, chiles, and herbs and places them on top of the noodles, with a squeeze of lime and more seasonings as desired.

Makes 4-6 servings.

Note: This is almost a meal on its own, and is traditionally eaten as breakfast, lunch or as a snack at any time of the day. For more-cooked steak, cook it in the boiling broth a few minutes.

—CHICKEN NOODLE SOUP—

2 tablespoons vegetable oil
4 shallots, sliced
1 clove garlic, chopped
8 oz. chicken thigh meat, shredded
4 oz. raw peeled shrimp
3 stalks celery, sliced
½ teaspoon sugar
2 tablespoons chopped green onions
2 tablespoons fish sauce
Salt and freshly ground black pepper
4½ cups chicken broth
9 oz. dried rice sticks, cooked in boiling water 4-5
    minutes, drained
2 tablespoons crushed peanuts
Cilantro leaves, to garnish

Heat oil in a wok or frying pan and stir-fry shallots and garlic about 30 seconds until fragrant. Add chicken and shrimp, stir-fry 1 minute, then add the celery and cook, stirring, 2 minutes. Add sugar, about half of the green onions and fish sauce, and season with salt and pepper. Blend well and set aside.

Bring chicken broth to a rolling boil with the remaining green onions and fish sauce. Place a portion of rice sticks in each of 4 individual serving bowls, put some chicken, shrimp and celery on top, then pour the broth over the top. Garnish with peanuts and cilantro and serve hot, with additional seasonings if desired.

Makes 4 servings.

FRUIT SALAD

½ cup sugar
1½ cups water
½ small watermelon or a whole honeydew melon
4-5 different fruits (fresh or canned), such as
    pineapple, grapes, lychees, rambutan, banana,
    papaya, mango or kiwi fruit
Crushed ice cubes

Make a syrup by boiling together the sugar
and water, then let cool.

Slice off about 3 inches off the top of melon,
scoop out flesh, discarding seeds, and cut
flesh into small chunks. Prepare all the other
fruits by cutting them into small chunks the
same size as the melon chunks.

Fill melon shell with the fruit and syrup.
Cover with plastic wrap and chill in the
refrigerator at least 2-3 hours. Serve on a bed
of crushed ice.

Makes 4-6 servings.

Note: If using canned fruit with syrup or
natural juice, you can use this instead of
making syrup for the dessert.

LYCHEE SORBET

1 lb. fresh lychees in their shells or 6 oz. canned
   lychees
½ cup syrup, page 93
Mint sprigs, to decorate

Peel fresh lychees and remove seeds. Place
the lychees in a food processor or blender
with the syrup and process to a smooth
puree.

Pour the puree into a freezerproof container
and place in the freezer about 2 hours or
until almost set.

Break up the iced mixture and whip until
smooth. Return mixture to the freezer 30-45
minutes to set until solid. Serve the sorbet
decorated with mint leaves.

Makes 4-6 servings.

Variation: 2 teaspoons root ginger can be
added to the sorbet mixture before blending,
if desired.

COCONUT CUSTARD

2 cups coconut milk
4 eggs, beaten
½ cup sugar
Edible flower petals, and/or exotic fruit, to decorate

In a medium bowl, blend the coconut milk, eggs and sugar. Beat until the sugar has completely dissolved and the mixture is smooth.

Pour mixture into a large serving bowl or 4 individual bowls, and place in a steamer over boiling water. Steam over high heat about 20 minutes if in a large serving bowl; 10-12 minutes if in 4 individual bowls.

Serve the custard warm or cold, decorated with petals or fruit.

Makes 4 servings.

Variation: A few drops of rosewater or any other fruit flavoring can be blended with the coconut milk to give extra flavor to the custard.

INDEX